From Suburbia to Subukia

From Suburbia to Subukia

by

Christine Matthews

AVON BOOKS
1 DOVEDALE STUDIOS
465 BATTERSEA PARK ROAD
LONDON SW11 4LR

Cover photographs:
Black and white English view by John Simcock.
East African view by Christine Matthews

Printed and bound in the U.K.

Avon Books

London

First Published 1996

ISBN 1 86033 995 6

For My Family

Acknowledgments

I cannot possibly thank everybody who has helped me to produce this book, but special thanks are due to: Anne Spoerry for her tremendous help and wonderful friendship over the years, and for writing the foreword; Nicky Blundell-Brown for steering me through those early times and for making it possible for me to have so many rewarding years; Nancy Maksud for arranging many of my trips in Africa, Graeme Backhurst and David Balston for the use of their photographs; Dinah and Nelson Kivuti of the CPK Guest House, Nairobi, for making me so very welcome on so very many occasions; Alexander Héroys of AMREF's UK office for his contribution to the final chapter of this book, and for all his help and encouragement throughout; all my friends both in Africa and the United Kingdom who encouraged me to set about writing this book in the first place, and special thanks to my son Chris who has spent many hours preparing proofs for publication.

Contents

Foreword

I cannot recall the very first time we met, but like swallows in spring Christine Matthews returned to Nairobi every other year to keep up with the work of AMREF.

She loved to come on my rounds, and we flew together to the deserts of the Northern frontier, to the border of Ethiopia, to the islands of Lamu on the Indian Ocean or joined sisters Robbie and Rosemary in their Masai Mobile Unit.

Fascinated by the local tribes, she was always ready for adventure; undaunted, she cared for nomadic children and helped to feed them in times of severe draught.

It was great fun to take Christine around. She was fascinated by the 'plane, but obviously a little unhappy to be flown by an old pilot like myself; she believed that it would be safer if she learned to fly herself so as to be able at least to land the 'plane should I have a heart attack. She went ahead and became one of that small and select fraternity of those who have taken off and landed a 'plane completely alone. Luckily for both of us she never had to take over from me but I am sure her achievement gave her great pleasure and added confidence.

Christine loved Subukia and my small farmhouse with its pink brick walls covered with jasmine. For her it was a home from home in Africa, a place where she could rest from her travels and where she will always be welcomed with open arms by Ndeto, Njununa, Joseph Munyasa and the others who have been running my farm for the last thirty years.

'Come again, Christine', or, as we say in Swahili, 'Karibu tena Subukia'.

Anne Spoerry MD DTM
Nairobi, Kenya - 1995

Twelve hundred million men are spread
About this Earth, and I and You
Wonder, when You and I are dead,
What will those luckless millions do?

Rudyard Kipling
from 'The Last Department'

Introduction

AMREF, The African Medical and Research Foundation, (originally the East African Flying Doctor Service) was the brainchild of Michael Wood, a British surgeon.

Michael, who had qualified as a doctor in 1943, during the grim years of the second world war, gained his early experience in surgery operating on bomb victims in Swindon as a member of an emergency operating team.

As a child Michael had always suffered severely from asthma, and his early years had been severely hampered by this condition. He later formed a deep-rooted interest in the African continent, and when, following his admission to the Royal College of Surgeons in 1946, he and his young wife Susan found an opportunity to travel to Mombasa aboard a Greek steamer this turned out to be a double bonus. The climate of East Africa, and its high altitude, proved to be the perfect antidote to Michael's asthma, and he was also able to pursue his interest in the African continent from first hand. Very soon Michael had accepted a six-month engagement with a specialist surgeon in Nairobi, and the experience gained here gave him a keen and life-long interest in the medical needs of the population of East Africa.

An early experience, gained whilst accompanying a medical colleague in a chartered aircraft in an attempt to bring medical help to the manager of a trading company in Somaliland, was sufficient proof to Michael that only by the establishment of a Flying Doctor Service, along the lines of that already operating in Australia, could the needs of the East African population be met. Within a very short time he had learned to fly - under the expert instruction of two second world war flying instructors - and very soon he was a qualified pilot.

Two other surgeons found themselves in East Africa at that time. One was Sir Archibald McIndoe, knighted in 1947 following his magnificent work during the recent war in treating burn victims, and the other was Tom Rees, a young American surgeon and a colleague of McIndoe. By the grace of God and providence these three met at Nairobi airport late in 1955, and through them was born the East African Flying Doctor Service.

This is only a very brief summary of a very long story, and the history of the foundation of what is now AMREF has already been told by others far more suitably qualified to do so than I am. Suffice it to say that following initial discussions with Sir Archibald McIndoe and Tom Rees Michael went out to Australia to see the flying doctor service there, to get some tips about the terrain and the organisation of a flying doctor service generally. He also discussed the project with Albert Schweitzer, since he was keen to learn about operating on leprosy. (Incidentally, in his first book, 'Go an extra mile', he tells of how Schweitzer sought his help with an operation for elephantiasis. Michael did the operation, but hadn't got the right instruments - and so he used seventy razor blades!)

And then he started off - one man with one 'plane and a lot of faith. Obviously it is no use flying anywhere if you can't land the 'plane at the other end, so local inhabitants were taught to level out landing grounds, make air strips, and so on. And it grew. At first most of the staff and doctors were Europeans, but gradually people elected by their tribes were brought in and trained to look after their own people. Later Michael was joined by Dr. Anne Spoerry, a French Doctor who was also a qualified pilot, and who took control of what is now called the mobile unit - which was responsible for the building of landing strips, field medical units and the like.

Over the years the organisation grew remarkably, so that now it incorporates not only emergency treatment (both medical and surgical) but also health education, nutrition education, family planning, famine relief - in fact practically every branch of medical science. The organisation also undertakes the training of elected representatives of the various tribes. These representatives are trained in medical procedures so that they can help to be responsible for looking after their own people.

Another important area of African life to which AMREF has made a substantial and lasting contribution is that of primary education. The bush schools, for instance, are situated in remote areas, far from the nearest main centres of population, and there is little if any funding from central government. Even the most elementary facilities, such as the provision of water supplies and basic sanitation, have in most cases to be left to the schools themselves. There are many instances where AMREF has stepped in to fulfil such needs, and my mind in particular goes to a small primary school at Kimuka, in the Ngong hills, where AMREF has funded the building of latrines and water storage tanks which have done much to ease the problems of the staff and pupils. Readers will learn more of the wonderful work of this particular school later in these pages.

When I first went out to Africa there was one 'prefab', with EAST AFRICAN FLYING DOCTOR SERVICES written along the fascia. Since then the organisation has changed out of all recognition. It now even has a workshop to make artificial limbs!

All this, then, was the product of just one man's vision. Michael Wood did not call it 'visionary', but it is interesting to note that he called his first book *Go an Extra Mile*, which is, of course, a quotation from St. Matthew's Gospel. 'When a man asks you to go with him a mile, go with him two'. There have, in fact, been three books to date published about AMREF - *Angels on Runway Zero Seven*, by Barry Wynne - and the two books written by Michael Wood himself - *Go an Extra Mile* and his most recent book which is called *Different Drums*. They are all fascinating books, and well worth reading.

This book tells the story of how I first became involved in the work of this remarkable organisation, and of how, as a result, I have had the most rewarding twenty years that any woman could possibly hope for. I hope that it will excite the reader's interest, and my greatest hope is that it may inspire anybody who feels ‘tired of life’ that there is always a new beginning just around the corner.

There was for me, anyway - and I am quite sure that there can be for you.

Sir Michael Wood
founder of the AMREF organization

Chapter One

A Triple Miracle

It is often said that 'life begins at forty.' Not for me, it didn't. There is no doubt about it - for me life began at sixty-one!

Before that it could hardly be said that I had led a very interesting life. It had not been particularly dull, and it had certainly had its moments. Bringing up two young children through the second world war, with a husband away on active service, could, I suppose, have been considered a challenge of a sort. Nor was this my first experience of war - I am just old enough to remember that first conflict of the century. I have a vivid recollection of playing in our garden in Surrey, at the age of about seven, when a Zeppelin appeared, looking rather pretty with the sun shining on it overhead. My anxious mother hurried me indoors - much to my disappointment - and the following day I wrote to my elder brother, at prep school, what must have been one of the shortest letters I ever penned. It read: *'Dear Geoff, Saw a Zepp! Love Sis.'*

I had a fairly conventional education at a girls' boarding school near London. I do not think I was particularly academic, and I always longed to be out on the playing fields rather than stuck in the classroom, but I did manage to matriculate with reasonable grades. After leaving school I was desperately keen to make a career in nursing; I have always been fascinated with medical science, and I really did think that I would be a good and efficient nurse and thereby make some sort of contribution to society. Much to my disappointment, this was not to be. My parents, as was I think common amongst their generation, did not think nursing a 'suitable' occupation for a young girl and firmly discouraged me from any such ambition. They did, however, feel that I should train for a career, and I was trained as a teacher of dancing. I was never very keen on this idea, but it did serve as a career of a sort. After qualifying I taught dancing, mainly to small children, for some years.

My life thereafter followed a fairly conventional pattern - marriage and children - (two sons, followed shortly after the second world war by a daughter who, unlike me, did qualify as a nurse) - and, later, a new and enjoyable role as a grandmother. But certainly my life was no more, and probably no less, exciting than that of the average housewife and mother.

Until, that is, I attained the magic age of sixty-one. That, as I have said, is when life really started for me in earnest.

It all began with what I have often called my 'triple miracle'.

It was 1971. I'd lost my second husband, my eldest son had recently suffered a fatal accident in Ethiopia and I was in a strange place; I'd had to move, and I was miserable. I don't think I'd ever felt lower in my life.

Maybe at such times one becomes more receptive - I don't know. But I was praying and praying for something useful to do, because I saw so many object lessons all round me - ladies who just sit and knit and do nothing else, and who get bored and boring; and I said : 'God, for goodness sake give me something useful to do.'

I went into the library one day, just looking for a book. This led to miracle number one. I didn't really know what I wanted, but I saw a book which was lying across the top of the fiction books. It hadn't been put away properly - it should have been on the non-fiction shelves. It had a picture of an aeroplane on the spine. I've always been interested in aeroplanes, so I thought this might be quite interesting. The book was entitled *Angels on Runway Zero Seven*, and was an account of the beginning of what is now AMREF, the African Medical and Research Foundation, (then the East African Flying Doctor Service), from the day it was inaugurated. Each chapter concerned a different stage in its history. I was absolutely fascinated by this book. It seemed funny to me - every time I picked it up I seemed to get a push - 'follow this up, follow this up.'

I didn't take the book back to the library until it was overdue. I kept on reading it and still getting this feeling about it. I even spoke to my church Minister about it. I said to him: 'I don't know, I think I'm going nuts. I seem to think that God's telling me to go and work for the flying doctors in Africa!' He asked me whether they had a London address, and when I confirmed that they had he said : 'Well, go and offer them some of your time. You'll soon find out whether or not you're going nuts.'

Taking my courage in both hands, I telephoned the AMREF London Office, and I was invited to visit the office and meet some of the staff. At this stage I had no fixed idea about what - if anything - I could possibly do for them. In any event, I thought, it would be a day out. Better than staying at home knitting, anyway!

When I arrived at the office I was introduced to Nicola Blundell-Brown, the London office secretary, who subsequently became AMREF's International Co-ordinator at their head office in Nairobi. This turned out to be the beginning of what has become a long and lasting friendship.

I don't think Nicola quite knew what to do with me on that first meeting. I helped her with a bit of 'dogsbody work' - filling envelopes, packing parcels, licking stamps and generally trying to help. In the course of conversation Nicola told me that Dr. Michael Wood (the founder of the whole organisation, who by this time was my hero) was coming up to a big board meeting in London, and she asked me if I would like to sit in on this meeting. This was an opportunity not to be missed, and so naturally I said I would love to attend the meeting. Obviously I was told that I would only be an observer and would not be allowed to speak, but the opportunity of actually meeting the great man himself more than compensated for this. For me, this was miracle number two.

So off I went up to this big board meeting - feeling very much a fish out of water - and I sat and listened to everything. Just before the meeting I had been introduced to a gentleman who had been responsible for fund raising in the United Kingdom. He had told me that for various reasons he was proposing to announce his resignation. He was given big 'thank you' for his work, and after this a little gremlin got into me. I said: 'Excuse me, Michael. I know I'm not supposed to say anything, but could I ask a question?' He said of course I could, and so I said: 'Who's going to do this for you now?'

'Oh,' he said, 'we'll have to give it up in England. We can't afford to pay anybody, and nobody's going to do it voluntarily. Why do you ask?'

I told him that I wanted to go and see my son's grave in Ethiopia, and I said that I thought I might go down to Kenya and see some of their work, and then perhaps give a talk or two for them. And then I thought to myself: 'You silly clot, what have you let yourself in for? You've never given a talk in your life, you don't know how to begin or what to say, and what are you going to use for money to get to Africa anyway?'

In any event, I thought 'I've done it now. I'd better go and see my bank manager.' So off I went to see the bank manager, who told me that I shouldn't even consider starting without at least £700. (The fare alone would be more than that now, but still, that is what he put as the basic). I said to him: 'I've said I'll go, so I must go. What do you advise me to do? Sell something, or borrow it, or what?' He said: 'Come and see me on Wednesday, and I'll see what I can sort out for you.'

And then came miracle number three. On the following Tuesday I got a letter from my late parents' solicitors to say that the gardener's cottage, which I had forgotten all about and which had been left to the man for his lifetime, had now been sold and they were happy to enclose a cheque for my share of the proceeds. How much do you think it was? £750. They say God always gives you a little extra! So I had a cheque for £750 - enough to get me to Africa, and with a little to spare. I drew out a few more of my savings, since I also wanted to visit my son's grave in Ethiopia, and back I went to the London office.

I told Nicola that I wished to go out to Africa, see some of the work, and get some information which I could incorporate into whatever talks I was going to give when I came back again. At that stage I didn't have a clue as to how I was going to organise all this - I suppose I just left it all in the hands of God. Nicola gave me some advice about tickets, travel arrangements, and the rest. She also said that she would notify AMREF in Nairobi that I was coming, so that they would be prepared to receive this strange lady and possibly send me out on some trips with the flying doctors. I also asked Nicola for advice as to where I could stay, at a reasonable price, and she recommended a hotel which was way up the Uhuru highway, a big highway in the centre of Nairobi. 'Uhuru,' incidentally, is Swahili for 'freedom'.

Nicola arranged with the Nairobi office for me to be booked into this hotel for an appropriate amount of time. So all that remained was for me to buy my air ticket and book a flight. I gave the AMREF London office details of my flight arrangements, packed my bags, and set off for Heathrow - and Africa. It was as simple as that!

And that was the start of over twenty years of visiting Africa, and travelling all over England in my little mini raising money for AMREF. A triple miracle indeed, and one which transformed my life.

A life which - for me - started at the tender age of sixty-one!

Chapter Two

First Steps in Africa

Christine Matthews. Widow - 61 years of age. No previous experience in anything to do with medicine (although, as I have said, it had been my early ambition to go into nursing) - and no knowledge of Africa apart from a brief holiday at the age of seventeen. No experience whatsoever in public speaking - the nearest I had ever got to that was occasionally reading the lesson in church and some infrequent appearances on stage with the local dramatic society! And here I was, on a jet bound for Nairobi, having volunteered to help the flying doctors and to give fund-raising lectures for them on my return. No wonder I said to myself, more than once on that first journey to Africa, 'Christine, what have you let yourself in for?'

After passing through customs at Nairobi airport I got a taxi to the hotel. As I have said, this hotel was way up the Uhuru highway, outside the city centre, and even the taxi driver had never heard of it. He had the most awful job finding it!

Eventually I arrived and checked in. The hotel was almost entirely occupied by business people - there seemed to be no tourists or foreign guests at all, and I felt somewhat out of place. I was certainly the only English person.

On arrival at the hotel I telephoned AMREF's offices at Wilson airport, Nairobi, and it was arranged that I should be taken out on a routine flight the following day. I was to make my own way to the airport the following morning, and there meet one of their pilots. All further arrangements would be made at that stage. It seemed that things were moving fast for me - and after lunch I decided to spend what was likely to be one of my rare free afternoons relaxing in the garden and enjoying the African sun.

Before very long the waiter who had served me with my meal came up to me and told me that he was an artist, and that he was having an exhibition of his pictures at the hotel that afternoon. He asked whether I would like a preview. So I sat on the lawn of the hotel and he surrounded me with a big circle of his pictures. Of course, I was a captive audience. I really had no alternative but to buy one! That, then, was my first purchase in Africa. I still have that picture on my living room wall. It is an oil painting depicting two Masai people drawing water from a stream, and I am very fond of it indeed. It cost me a whole £5 - not bad for a lasting memento of my first ever trip to Africa. I shall always treasure it.

The following morning I took a taxi down to the hangar at the airport, where I was met by an AMREF pilot. He told me that he was going to take me out on a routine flight to Mwanza, which is a town on the shores of Lake Victoria. There he had to pick up a patient and transport him to a big hospital in Nairobi. This, then, was to be my first flight in an AMREF 'plane, and I could hardly contain my excitement.

We didn't see anything of Mwanza itself, since we had no occasion to leave the airstrip. We taxied as near as possible to the route leading to the Mwanza Bush Hospital, the patient was brought out, and he was loaded into the aeroplane on a stretcher. I never did discover precisely what was wrong with him - I don't think it was anything very dramatic - but he had some illness or other which necessitated him being taken to a bigger hospital with better facilities. So back we flew to Nairobi, and delivered him to Kenyatta hospital in Nairobi. This is a fine, big hospital. Our only trouble occurred on our arrival at the hospital, when nobody could locate a wheelchair or any other means of conveying him to his bed. However, eventually a trolley was found and the man was duly delivered to the ward where he was to be treated. We all breathed a sigh of relief, not least - I have no doubt - the patient himself!

There was nothing very remarkable about this trip, except that it was my very first trip flying with AMREF in Kenya. Little did I know, at that time, that it was to be only the first of many, many such flights. However, then it was all a totally new experience for me. I was, of course, very interested to see the terrain over which we were flying. This seemed pretty bare - I don't remember seeing many animals on that first trip apart from enormous herds of impala and zebra - which are to be seen everywhere in East Africa. I was, however, interested to observe what looked to me like some circles on the ground. These turned out to be Masai villages. The Masai villagers live in 'Manyattas,' little adobe houses. Their villages are in very isolated areas, surrounded by circular thorn hedges, and virtually all that can be seen from the air are these circular villages with a lot of Masai cattle.

Although I was not to know it at the time I was, over the course of the next twenty years, to see a great deal of these nomadic Masai tribesmen and their families, and I have over this time come to form a tremendous admiration for these proud, dignified, wandering people. Contrary to popular misconception the Masai are not 'warriors' in the accepted sense of the word although they will, of course, fight when necessary to protect their families and property. Their traditional pastoral, nomadic way of life was severely disrupted by European colonisation at the end of the nineteenth century, when the authorities endeavoured to impose upon them agricultural disciplines foreign to their culture and way of life. The Masai, in common with several other groups including the Fulani of West Africa and the Dinka of the Nile Sudd in Ethiopia, are essentially a pastoral people; to the Masai his cattle are both his livelihood and his status symbol. They are also the main source of his food in the form of milk, sometimes mixed with blood for nutriment. Historically they used to follow regular migration patterns in which, after the rains, they took their herds from the best land to the more arid areas so as to take advantage of the new growth, later to return to the richer pastures to enable them to survive until the next rainy season. When the nineteenth century colonists reallocated much Masai land for cultivation this pattern was severely disrupted, with the consequence that the Masai have been left to struggle on poor pastures.

These, then, are the people I came over the years to know and respect so well. I have been entertained by Masai families in their little Manyattas, and - as will be seen later in this book - on one occasion was presented with a little Masai stool and necklace to use as visual aids on my lectures. So much for the fierce, warlike Masai tribespeople about whom we hear so much fiction!

But I digress.

When we alighted from the 'plane at the AMREF hangar at Wilson airport I asked the pilot whether there was any hope of going anywhere else that day. By this time I was simply raring to go, and wanted to fly here, there and everywhere all at the drop of a hat! Disappointingly, but understandably, I was told by the pilot that it was not for him to arrange trips for visitors. He advised me to go back to my hotel and arrange matters by phoning AMREF from there. Just then he turned round and saw someone entering the hangar.

'Oh look,' he said, 'here's Dr. Spoerry. I am sure you would like to meet her.' 'Anne,' he said, 'this is Christine Matthews from England.'

Another miracle! I had read about the famous Dr. Spoerry in the book which had sparked off this great adventure, and by this time I had formed such an admiration for her that she really loomed as one of my heroines. Born in Cannes towards the end of the first world war, Anne studied medicine in France. Her studies were, however, severely disrupted by the second world war, and when, finally, those dreadful war years were at last over and Europe settled down to an uneasy peace Anne completed her studies in Paris.

Wishing to break free from the desolation of post-war Europe and to shed the bitter memories of the war Anne decided to make a new life for herself in Africa. The war had given her a keen insight into the needs of the oppressed masses, and for fifteen years following her arrival in Africa she combined a busy general practice with farming. Over this period she became keenly aware of the desperate need for medical treatment and health education in the remote areas of the African bush. How to set about this undertaking, however, was quite another matter. The vast distances involved seemed to pose an insuperable problem.

When, in the early 1960s, she came to hear of Michael Wood and his East African Flying Doctor Service she did not hesitate. She sold her farm, met Michael Wood, learned to fly, bought a Cherokee 235 and in 1965 she placed herself and her machine at the disposal of the Service. Over the years she built up what is now called the 'mobile unit' and today, at the age of seventy-seven, she still remains a driving force behind the foundation. To this day she still continues to make regular forays to her clinics in the African bush.

This, then, was the background of the woman about whom I had read so much and for whom I had formed such an admiration. And now I was about to shake hands with her. No wonder I was thrilled!

'Hello,' she said, 'and what are you doing out here, all the way from England?' I told her what I had in mind.

'Like to come out with me?' she asked.

Well, of course, I could imagine nothing better. I had never dreamed of such luck! 'Oh, Dr. Spoerry,' I said, 'I would indeed.'

'Be down here at eight o'clock in the morning,' she said, 'and I'll take you out with me.'

And that was the beginning of what has become a long and beautiful friendship. How lucky I was that on this, my first trip to Africa, I should - quite by chance - have met Dr. Spoerry herself and been given this wonderful opportunity to see her at work. Or was it chance? I often wonder. These things often seem to be part of a larger plan, and certainly I am sure that the success of my work for AMREF over the next twenty years owes a great deal to that chance, first meeting with my friend Anne Spoerry.

Promptly at eight o'clock the following morning I was again 'on parade' at Wilson airport. Anne was waiting for me and off we went in her little 'plane - a Piper Cherokee. We flew to Amboseli, in Kenya, and landed at a little landing strip right inside the Amboseli Game Park.

It was here that I first learned a local legend about flying small aeroplanes in the African bush. It is sometimes said that you should protect the tyres of the 'plane with branches of thorn trees, because the hyenas like the taste of rubber - which isn't very good for your tyres. Nor, I suppose, would be the thorn trees if pressed too hard into the tyres, so it has to be done quite carefully - but at least it is better than having your tyres eaten by hyenas!

We walked to a small clinic which was just near the airstrip, where Anne spent a large portion of the morning treating women and their babies. I remember spending quite a lot of time holding these babies while they were given their injections. They wriggled a bit, but by and large they were pretty well behaved. The clinic undertakes general medical treatment for people living nearby, and for Anne it was very much a routine trip. Not for me, however. For me it was another 'first' - my first real experience of medicine in the bush. It was wonderful to think that I was really able to make myself useful - if only by holding wriggling babies!

There was a young African in charge of the clinic, and he was in trouble because he had apparently not kept his records properly. Anne was very cross with him, and barked at him like a sergeant major! I felt rather sorry for this young man - I would not like to get on the wrong side of Anne Spoerry, who can when necessary be a very efficient disciplinarian.

After spending the remainder of the morning at this clinic Anne took me to an early lunch at the restaurant at the game lodge, and we sat on a veranda outside, looking at the animals. All the time I was fascinated by an elephant, which was wandering round and round the area. The elephant seemed fairly tame, and apparently it came here to raid the dustbins in search of tit-bits. However, I was told that somebody had nearly got into serious trouble for patting this elephant and generally treating it like a domestic dog. That, of course, would have been too much for any self-respecting, proud African elephant to bear, and so it had got rather cross. For this reason there was a strict injunction against making intimate advances to this particular elephant. They say that an elephant never forgets, and I am sure this one would never have forgotten it if I had done so!

Incidentally, later in my travels, when I returned to Amboseli on another occasion, I met a lady who was investigating this particular herd and carrying out some research into what is called 'musth' - an aspect of the reproductive cycle of elephants. She knew the names of all the elephants in the herd, and she really did earn my admiration.

After lunch we bade our farewells to the staff at the Amboseli bush hospital and flew back to Wilson airport. I returned feeling tired but very elated - I really did, by now, feel that I was contributing something to the work of the flying doctors, rather than being merely just another tourist.

We arrived back at the hangar at Wilson airport at about 2 o'clock in the afternoon and somebody said to me: 'There's someone waiting to see you, Mrs. Matthews.' I said 'Who? I don't know anybody out here.' I was told that it was a gentleman with a big limousine. Shortly afterwards a gentleman came up to me and said: 'I've come from the Manager of Nile Star, who wants to see you in the office.'

Nile Star is a tourist organisation, and I had booked a week with them to join a game park safari in Uganda. This was to have been the following week. I was taken to the office, and the gentleman said: 'Mrs Matthews, you're booked on our tour next week, but can you go today instead?' 'Why?' I asked. He explained that if I could go today there was a nice couple who could go with me, and also a very interesting geography professor and his wife who would join our party in Uganda, and he was sure that I would love that. I said: 'Yes, but for heavens sake, all my gear's at the hotel, and what time would I have to go?' He told me that he'd got all that organised and said: 'I knew you'd say yes' - (I hadn't, then). But he said that he'd contacted my hotel, and that they would put a bathroom and everything at my disposal and keep my room for me until my return.

I was told that I could only take a flight bag for this week, so the hotel would lock up my luggage, and there would be a hairdresser if I wanted one. I really did feel that I was getting the VIP treatment, and felt very honoured!

I asked what time I had to be ready, and he said he would pick me up in his private car at 5 o'clock, which would give me time for a rest. 'And meanwhile,' he said, 'here's your lunch.' In came a big tray of sandwiches. So much for travelling alone and not being looked after! True to his word the gentleman arrived at my hotel at 5 o'clock and drove me down to the airport - none of this hanging around at an airport for 2 hours for Christine Matthews! - no, not that day.

And this led to what turned out to be one of the most hilarious and hair-raising experiences in all my time in Africa - though it did not seem quite so funny at the time. When giving talks about my travels I have often referred to it as my experience of 'Involuntary Evangelism at 30,000 feet.'

And it all happened on my flight to Uganda.

Chapter Three

Ugandan Safari

On arrival at Nairobi airport I was taken straight to the 'plane - a Douglas DC10 - and was introduced to the young couple who were to accompany me on the tour of the Ugandan game parks. Paul and Phyllis seemed a very pleasant couple, and we settled down in the 'plane for the short flight to Entebbe airport.

We were very lucky. The 'plane was by no means full. We had the front six seats all to ourselves. I was very glad eventually that we did have the front six seats, for reasons which will come to light later. I had the three seats one side and Paul and Phyllis had the three seats the other side, so we could talk across to each other, which was very pleasant. We were due to land at Entebbe at eight o'clock.

By eight o'clock we were practically over Entebbe, but there seemed to be some sort of delay in landing. We flew round and round the airport, wondering what was going on. We kept looking at our watches. 'Long time stacking,' we thought. After a while the pilot's voice came over the intercom. He said that he was very sorry about the delay, but they couldn't get the landing wheels down. The crew came and got the carpets and floorboards up all down the centre of the 'plane, and all this time we were circling round and round over the enormous expanse of Lake Victoria. It looked like a very watery grave indeed!

Have you ever seen under the floorboards of a jet? You know what the inside of a television's like - or where they dig up all the telephone wires? All we could see was a solid mass of cables and wires. How they ever knew what they were looking for I don't know. After what seemed an age they put the floorboards and carpets down again, and we flew round some more. Still there seemed to be no sign of landing.

Poor Phyllis was getting extremely nervous. She was one of the very nervy kind, and she was doing a bit of sobbing already. Then the pilot said that he thought the landing wheels were down but they couldn't tell because the indicator light was not showing. They were going to fly around the control tower so that the control staff could put the binoculars on us to see if the wheels were down. So much for high technology!

By this time Phyllis really was getting in a real panic. She seemed convinced that we were all going to die, and I was doing my best to calm her down. 'Oh, stow it, Phyllis,' I said. 'I said my prayers last night, and I am sure you did as well. You'll see - we'll be alright. There's nothing to worry about.'

And then the intercom crackled into action again, and the pilot explained that our lights were blinding the control staff and they couldn't see, so we'd got to shut off our lights and fly around in the dark!

This really was too much for Phyllis altogether, and by this time she was nearly hysterical. I was still doing my best to calm her down. I can't remember precisely what I said, - but whatever it was didn't seem to have the desired effect. She had totally lost control of herself. Eventually I said: 'Now look here, Phyllis, I know perfectly well that God sent me out here to do this work for the flying doctor service. I've only just started, and I'm quite sure He's not going to scarper the whole idea by killing me off before I've even begun! You can be absolutely sure that this plane's going to be alright.' I don't altogether know whether I was as confident as I sounded; I like to think I was.

By then we had our lights on again and the pilot said that the landing wheels were down but they weren't locked, and so he would attempt a landing but it might be very noisy. By this time the stewardess had come round to drill us in emergency procedures and to prepare us for an emergency landing.

I was in trouble with that stewardess because I'd flatly refused to take my false teeth out. I was much more frightened of waking up in hospital without my false teeth than I was of being killed! Eventually I decided that it would be much easier to take my teeth out and put them back again as soon as she had gone. At last the pilot announced he was going to attempt a landing, the 'plane started to descend and we all braced ourselves for the impact.

And then up we went again!

'Sorry about that,' said the pilot. 'I wasn't sure we'd got the wings completely level.' Again this happened, and round we came again. We seemed to be playing a game of 'ring a ring o' roses' in mid-air! I need hardly explain what state poor Phyllis was in by this time.

But the third time we did land. And it was very noisy. However this time the pilot did manage to keep the plane level. I don't know what happened to the luggage in the hold, and I was very thankful that I had been told only to travel with hand luggage. People who had luggage in the hold would probably have lost it all.

There was foam on the runway, fire-engines - the lot. I was thankful I didn't have to come down the chute. As I have said, I was glad we were in the front seats. We could climb straight out on to the wing, where we came down the fireman's ladder. I have always wanted to come down a fireman's ladder - another ambition fulfilled! And we were ferried in to the terminal on fire-engines, ambulances, - whatever was available. I don't think any of us very much minded how we got there - we were just thankful to be alive.

Immigration was chaos. We were about an hour and a half late, but better late than never. Phyllis was still on the verge of hysterics, and I was still doing my best to calm her down. I don't think her husband was saying very much - I think he was a bit nonplussed.

As we were standing in this queue I felt a tap on my shoulder. I turned round, and there was an Indian gentleman in a black robe with white socks. Gravely, he bowed towards me. 'Madam,' he said, 'I want to thank you.' I was completely taken aback.

'Thank you very much,' I replied, 'but why?'

'Because,' he said solemnly, 'we all owe our lives to you.'

Honestly, I've never felt so embarrassed in my life! To cap it all Phyllis then went off into peals of laughter. Tears had turned to laughter; she was still quite hysterical. I kept on saying: 'Shut up, Phyllis, shut up.' It was all most embarrassing!

And then I said to the Indian gentleman: 'I don't know what I had to do with it. I think we all owe our lives to God.' He said: 'Maybe, but I was sitting behind you in the plane, and I heard every word you said. I am quite convinced that we owe all our lives to you.'

Of course I was stuck with the dear old fellow all through the immigration queue! It turned out that he had a tailoring business in Kampala, and he'd been into Nairobi on a buying session. He told me quite a lot about this, and apart from the embarrassing circumstances of our encounter he proved to be a very interesting companion.

It will be remembered that this was 1972 - the age of Idi Amin. Day by day harsher and harsher decrees were issuing forth from the dictator's headquarters in Kampala. It was, on reflection, perhaps not the best of times to go on Safari in Uganda.

All this happened on a Saturday. On the following Thursday Amin expelled all the Asians from Uganda. Ever since then I have wondered what became of my dear old gentleman who was so convinced that I'd saved his life, and who had ended up being turned out of his home country.

Somebody once suggested to me that he's probably a Christian by now. If so, that was VERY involuntary evangelism!

Representatives from Nile Star, the company responsible for our tour of the Ugandan game parks, were awaiting us at Entebbe, and apparently all this drama had caused quite a stir. We had become unwitting celebrities. The representatives had been in the control tower observing our circling 'plane, and the poor men had been having to prepare for the possibility that they would have to organise coffins for their clients instead of a relaxing holiday! We were introduced to these gentlemen after clearing through immigration, and also to our driver, who had travelled on the same 'plane from Nairobi. The driver was a very smart, dapper little African gentleman with an imperial beard, and I was highly amused to discover that his name was Cromwell!

The Nile Star representatives were so relieved to see us land safely that we were invited to one of their homes for dinner that evening, following which we were driven to our hotel in Kampala. The following day (Sunday) was to be a free day in Kampala, and we were scheduled to set off for our game park tour on the Monday. After the drama of the near air disaster I, for one, felt quite ready for a day off. The game park tour was to comprise six of us in all - Cromwell, the geography teacher and his wife, Paul, Phyllis, and myself.

When we all met on the Monday morning I was intrigued to notice that Cromwell had shaved off his beard. I said: ' What's happened to your beard, Cromwell? Didn't your girl friend like it?'

'Haven't you seen the papers?' he asked?

'No,' I replied, 'I'm on holiday, and I haven't seen any papers.' 'Orders went out this morning,' explained Cromwell, that every man in Uganda must be clean shaven. I wouldn't dare wear my beard after that!'

The next day, when we were in Mbarara, Cromwell said: 'Have you read the papers this morning?' I said: 'No, why?' He said: 'Well, you'll soon see some rather odd sights going on.'

It really was rather funny, although the reason wasn't funny. This was the time of mini-skirts, and the order had gone out from Amin that nobody must wear a skirt more than one inch above the knee.

And of course the policemen were all having a lovely time. There they were at every street corner with measuring tapes, measuring all the girls' legs! Everyone who didn't pass muster was taken in. The tourists were allowed to go. I don't know what happened to the Ugandans.

The game park excursions were fascinating. Certainly we were very lucky to have our friend the geography teacher with us; he taught us a lot. I remember him telling me a lot about the formation of the Ruwenzori mountains. Evidently he was prospecting suitable places to which to take parties of students for educational holidays. I believe that in the end he decided against Uganda for his students - mainly because this was the age of Idi Amin and the risks were considered to outweigh the educational benefits.

We set off in a small mini-van, and we drove through the most wonderful scenery - mostly forest and jungle. Uganda is extremely lush; at that time there was no sign of any drought at all. What struck me more than anything else was the proliferation of banana trees. On each side of the track there were rows and rows of these banana trees. Groups of baboons were having tea parties - or banana parties - in the middle of the road!

I enquired about the main exports from Uganda, and I was told, as expected, that they export such things as tea, coffee, cocoa and so forth.

'And bananas, of course,' I remarked.

'No,' I was told. 'We eat all those.'

I could believe this when I discovered that every single meal, at whatever time of day, started with matoke. Matoke, when served up, looks like a large scoop of very grey and unappetising looking mashed potato. Whatever else it contains, it is based on bananas. These are what they call 'cooking' bananas, or cooking plantains. As I said, matoke is served up everywhere, and the staff of the restaurants were very puzzled when I refused matoke - which I found absolutely horrible.

The banana trees were full of monkeys; green monkeys and, to my great delight, a great many of the black and white colobus monkeys. I was very relieved to learn that it is now illegal to kill these monkeys and use their skins for making rugs. In the past there was a considerable trade in these monkey skins, but now products made from colobus skin cannot be sold.

There were also enormous herds of elephant, and also of buffalo in the more open parts. Of course every herd of either elephant or buffalo has to have its leader. At one stage we had a large herd of buffalo on our left hand side and further on, to our right, was a large herd of elephant. As we passed the herd of buffalo their leader detached himself from the rest and stood right across the road behind us. Shortly we approached the elephants, and the leader of this herd detached herself and stood across the road in front of us - rocking from side to side and looking rather menacing! So there we were - unable to move either forwards or back. Eventually we edged forward gingerly, whereupon the elephants dispersed.

I was interested to observe, every time we passed a herd of elephant, that the babies were pushed into the middle of the herd for protection. All wild animals, but particularly elephants, are very protective to their young.

We also saw a tremendous proliferation of birds, and to me the birds in Africa are just as interesting as the wild animals. Many of these birds are very seldom seen outside Africa, even in a zoo. We saw many black and yellow weaver birds, lilac rollers, parrots of all kinds, secretary birds and - which I really loved - congregations of tiny malachite kingfishers. These are really beautiful - they look exactly like little glowing jewels flying around in the sun.

We did not see many snakes - most of these would have been hiding out in the undergrowth. However at one stage all traffic on the road was forced to a halt because an enormous python wanted to cross the road. Until that time I had never realised how big pythons could grow. This was a very large, slow-moving python, and it was just like waiting for a train at a level crossing. Some people got out to look at it, but I decided that on this occasion discretion was the better part of valour. I did not want it to be said that I had survived a near air disaster only to be crushed by a python! Eventually it got across the road and we moved on.

We were heading for Paraa game park, up towards the lakes, where we were to stay the night. On the way we passed by a swamp, and this swamp seemed to be solid with the backs of hippos. You know how they put their noses up to breathe. Little white egrets were using the backs of these hippos as bridges - walking on the backs of all these hippos. It just looked like an absolutely solid mass of egrets on walkabout! That fascinated me.

Later on we arrived in the vicinity of Lake George, where we boarded a small motor boat and took a trip up the river to the lake itself. This was an absolutely fascinating trip. I sat up at the front with the 'skipper,' who was very keen on the wildlife. He knew just where to find the most interesting sights. At one stage he took us right up a little inlet at the side of the river, because he said that he knew something interesting there to show us.

There was a mother hippo, tucked in the middle of the reeds, with a very small baby, which she was suckling. She seemed quite tame, and very pleased to be visited by us!

As we sailed up the river, again the bird life attracted me very much. There were more of the lovely, colourful little malachite kingfishers, African lily-trotters (Jacanas), stilts and goliath herons. All the way along the banks of the river were lying crocodiles in one solid line - without a single gap. They were all lying facing the river, with their jaws open. I was intrigued by this and asked why they were lying so. Apparently it is so that the little birds can run in and out of their mouths and pick their teeth, to keep them clean!

At intervals the crocodiles would slide into the water, near to the boat. There were a number of small children on board, and they kept climbing on to the rails and jumping up and down in excitement. I was terrified lest one of the children should tumble into the water and be devoured by a crocodile. Happily none of them did - at least not while I was looking!

We took this trip all the way to some falls up at the end of the river, which were very beautiful indeed. Here there were many more crocodiles, hippopotami and birds. Altogether it really was the most beautiful of nature trips.

Early in the evening we arrived at Paraa game lodge. As we turned in at the gates we could see a long drive leading up to the lodge itself, and beside the entrance gate was a little house. We were told that this was Queen Elizabeth's house. Apparently it had been built for the Queen Mother when she went out for a state visit. We drove up to the lodge, where we had our dinner, which - needless to say - started with matoke! However we were told that we would not be able to sleep in the lodge because there was not room for five. We would have to stay in Queen Elizabeth's house.

We didn't mind this at all - it added to the adventure. However, we were strictly forbidden from setting foot outside, and walking in the grounds. If we wanted to go out we would have to wait for Cromwell, and he would take us in the van.

After dinner Cromwell drove us down to the bungalow, where we were each given a set of two keys. There were three rooms in the house. One of our keys was for the front door and the other was for our respective bedrooms. There was one big main room, the sitting room, which had been converted, and there were two double rooms with facilities, one on each side of the main room. The two couples were to occupy the rooms to each side, and I was given the big main room.

I asked Cromwell where my bathroom was. He said: 'Ah, wait a minute, lady, and I will show you.' So we went out - I opened the front door with my key, and he took me round two sides of this house to a little lean-to, which had been converted into a perfectly adequate bathroom and toilet.

'That's all very well, Cromwell,' I said, 'but we have been told that we're not to set foot outside unless you're here.'

'Ah,' he replied, 'that is alright, lady. I will stay here until you go to bed. You won't want it until you're ready for bed. You won't want to come out in the night.'

'You don't know me, Cromwell!' I said.

So I had a look around, and there wasn't even a bucket or anything. So I thought; 'What do I do?' I decided to use it then, and not to lock the door. And if necessary, I thought, I shall just have to make a dash in the night.

In the middle of the night I was awakened by the most awful noises - grunting and shuffling and snorting - munching, it sounded like. I looked out of the window, and I think that every hippo out of the Paraa river had decided to camp out in the front of this bungalow. They were having a lovely time. It was bright moonlight, and I spent quite a long time watching them. I thought: 'This is fascinating.' Then I thought: 'Oh dear, suppose I have to go out to the loo?' Fortunately they didn't seem to be all round the house. They were moving parallel to the bungalow.

I watched them for what was beginning to seem an awful long time - getting a bit uncomfortable - when eventually they seemed to move away. So I thought; 'OK, now I can open the front door and go round. 'Suppose I find a hippo in the bathroom,' I thought! Then I realised how stupid I was being. They weren't coming up for water, they were coming up for grass, and there wasn't any grass in the bathroom! I'd got into a slightly nervous state by that time.

Eventually, when I did go out, what do you think I saw? I was absolutely face to face with an elephant. - A great big mother elephant, taking her baby for a walk. And this elephant had just decided that the creepers round the front door would taste rather nice! So I hastily shut the door, still feeling more and more uncomfortable, and eventually I peered out. She had wandered away, and I made a dash for it, and there wasn't a hippo in the bathroom. I came back and went to sleep again.

In the morning, while we were foregathering, I said to the others: 'Did you hear those hippos last night? Didn't they make a row!'

Our friend the geography professor, without even a suspicion of a smile on his face, said: 'Oh, they were hippos, were they? We thought it was you snoring'!

Despite having been mistaken for a hippopotamus I managed to struggle back on to the mini-bus and we set off back to Kampala, passing through the same glorious scenery as before. From Kampala we were to be transferred back to Entebbe for the return flight to Nairobi. I expected no problems in obtaining the return flight to Nairobi. I thought I'd already encountered quite enough flight problems for one trip!

Not a bit of it! Whilst I was waiting in the hotel for transport to the airport a representative of one of the English newspapers was arrested. There was clearly a crisis of some sort going on, and there seemed to be no method of getting a flight back from Entebbe to Nairobi. At one stage I had an awful vision of having to climb aboard an African train, where half the passengers sit on the roof! That would have been interesting, if nothing else!

Thankfully someone - I don't know who to this day - was able to pull some strings for me and I did get a seat on a 'plane back from Entebbe to Nairobi. When I arrived at Entebbe and finally boarded a 'plane I saw our fated Douglas DC10 still stranded on the runway. It had still not been moved. The country was in the most terrific crisis, and most of the available 'planes had been commandeered by wealthy Asians and politicians. One, I remember, was used to fly Geoffrey Rippon to Uganda.

However on this occasion, I am happy to say, our landing wheels did lock down, and we landed safely at Nairobi.

Very shortly after my return to Nairobi I was off on my travels again. As I have said, one of my purposes in going to Africa in the first place was to visit my son's grave in Addis Ababa, the capital of Ethiopia. In order to obtain a visa to visit Ethiopia it was necessary for me to remain there for ten days. I visited my son's grave in Addis Ababa, which I was pleased to note had been beautifully maintained. The British cemetery in Addis is a lovely place - open, with plenty of space, clean and very tidy. Friends of my late son had ensured that fresh flowers had been left on the grave on each anniversary of his birthday, which I thought very touching.

In the circumstances I did not wish to spend the whole ten days in Addis Ababa. I therefore booked a seat on a DC3 'plane, which does a 'triple hop' - flying from Addis to Gonder, and thence to Aksum, Lake Tana and back to Addis. On the day I was flying to Gonder a funeral was scheduled to start there. In Ethiopia a major funeral lasts for three days. This particular funeral was of a relative of the Emperor Haile Selassie, so it was a very major affair indeed. The funeral party wailed all the way to Gonder and all the way back again - which I found a bit trying. However it was all very colourful. All the Ethiopians were in their traditional dress and carrying the famous multi-coloured Ethiopian straw umbrellas.

I flew on, by way of Aksum, to Lake Tana - a big lake which is, incidentally, the source of the Blue Nile, which runs from Lake Tana to Khartoum, where it joins the White Nile at Omdurman. I took a trip on the lake, which is very beautiful, and I was intrigued to watch some boats being built of papyrus. In the centre of the lake is a big island. I was told that no women were allowed to land there, since it contains a monastery.

From Addis I flew back to Nairobi, where I had a brief opportunity to say my fond farewells to Anne Spoerry and all my new-found friends from AMREF before returning to England.

I felt that this, my first trip to Africa, had really been tremendously worthwhile. I had covered a lot of ground in a relatively short time, and as well as having had a great deal of fun, and some intriguing experiences, I had 'cut my teeth' on my work of helping AMREF. God had seen fit to spare me from a watery grave in Lake Victoria, and now, I reflected as I winged my way back to England, it was time to put all this to the test.

I had volunteered, however rashly, to give these fund-raising talks, but how I was going to set about it I really didn't know.

'God will help me,' I thought.

He did.

When my time for speaking was over I opened the meeting up for questions, and this was the big test. How would I fare? Not too badly, as it turned out. When the inevitable questions which I could not answer were put I resorted to the simple expedient of honesty, and this has never let me down in all my years as a speaker. When you just don't know - say it. Nobody will mind, and they will think all the more of you for your honesty!

I found a pattern of questioning at this meeting which was to be repeated many times in later years. Questions seemed to fall into two distinct categories, depending on the sex of the questioner. Women are always more interested in the medical and social aspects of AMREF's work, and in particular in how I came to want to travel so far abroad in the first place. The men, on the other hand, always ask difficult questions about aviation and the performance and specifications of the aeroplanes. I offer no prizes for guessing which category of questions I found most easy to handle. Although I did learn something of avionics when taking my flying lessons, this was much later; at that early stage my knowledge of the subject was precisely nil!

By and large I felt I had cause to be reasonably satisfied with that first talk, and quite a few of those present were interested enough to offer to pass on my name to their local churches and organisations as a potential speaker. I found this very encouraging.

This, of course, was only a very small first step, but at least it seemed to prove to me that I was going in the right direction. It was also a great boost to my own self-confidence. I had at least proved to myself that I could give a talk without drying up, passing out, or climbing under the nearest table to hide my embarrassment!

This did not, however, really solve the problem of how to publicise my proposed talks. Once again, I was helped by an unseen hand.

I was shopping in Sutton one day, not long after my talk to the church, and I was standing rather vaguely in Sutton High Street, wondering about this task which I taken upon myself. 'What do I do?' 'How do I begin?' 'Whom do I approach?' I was almost thinking these questions aloud. And then a voice seemed to say to me: 'look where you're standing.'

I looked round, and discovered that I was standing right outside the offices of the local newspaper, the *Sutton Herald*.

I walked into these offices, without quite knowing what to say, and there was a lady sitting at the front office desk.

'Would your newspaper,' I asked her, 'be prepared to put a little bit in about a lady who has just been to Africa to see the work of the flying doctor service, and who would like to give some talks about it?'

The response was immediate - and quite unexpected.

'Jim,' the lady called out, 'You've got a story here.'

So down came Jim. I think they must have been very short of copy that week, because they gave me about half a page and a photograph. They even sent one of their photographers to my flat in Sutton for this purpose. And so this article appeared in the *Sutton Herald* about a lady who gave these wonderful talks about the East African Flying Doctor Service - and apart from one brief chat to my local church I hadn't given a single talk at that time!

As a result of the publicity generated by the newspaper article and the contacts through my local church word generally got around. In what seemed like no time at all I discovered that somebody had put my name on a list of Womens' Institute speakers, somebody else had given my name to the Townswomens' Guild list, and it 'just all happened'!

Soon requests for talks were coming in by practically every post, from all sorts of places. It was all very good for my geography of Britain, because within no time at all I found myself touring the highways and byways of southern England, giving what in those days were still informal and unillustrated talks about the work of the flying doctors in East Africa. I really did seem to have made a very promising start. Later, as will be seen in a subsequent chapter, my talks incorporated slide presentations and were spread throughout the country - but these were as yet still early days.

I very soon found that I was booked for about two or three talks a week. It had got to the stage that every time I picked up the telephone I wondered where on earth I was going to be invited this time!

The problem arose as to how funds were to be raised for AMREF through these talks. That, after all, was the whole object of the exercise. I gave a great deal of thought to whether to charge for my talks or to ask for voluntary donations. I found this very difficult. Every organisation is different, and I never knew whether I was going to a tiny little Womens' Institute with practically no funds, or to - for instance - a Rotary Club, which might pay very well. It didn't seem to be fair to quote a fixed fee, since had I done so this would have had to be a standard fee, and would have to be pitched to the affordable level of the smallest of gatherings. Some small churches and meetings might only be able to afford a small fee of, say £3.00, whereas from a Rotary Club or a Trade Guild far more might be expected.

I therefore decided not to quote any fee at all, but merely to ask for either a donation to the Flying Doctor Service or for a collection to be organised. Obviously I also asked for a contribution to the cost of my petrol and travelling expenses. This seemed to work very well indeed. Some organisations are very generous when it comes to charity, and by and large I probably raised more funds this way than if I had quoted a fixed fee.

I still continued to pay frequent visits to the London office, where I was now beginning to become quite a popular visitor. Funds from my talks were beginning to roll into head office, and they were beginning to 'sit up and take notice' out in Nairobi. I still continued to help out in the office with the clerical work, and I remember on one occasion having to pack up an artificial limb to send out to Africa in a cardboard box. We even had to make the box!

However my thoughts were turning more and more to my fund-raising activities.

And here, I was running into a problem. I was beginning to run out of material.

I found that I was frequently being asked, during my talks, whether I had any pictures or slides available of the work of the organisation. On my trip to Africa I had not taken a single photograph. At that time I didn't even possess a camera, and anyway I had been far too busy nearly crashing in aeroplanes and being mistaken for hippopotami to give any thought to photography.

Also, I began to suspect that my talks might be in danger of becoming somewhat stale. All my talks to date seemed to be mere variations of my original, informal chat to my local church meeting. I had a strong feeling that some new impetus was required. I was also beginning to get re-bookings, and they would hardly be content with the same talk a second time. I couldn't really return to East Africa, but...

Or could I?

I was sitting at home one morning, pondering this problem, when the telephone sprang into action.

'Hello, Christine,' came a voice, 'this is Anne Spoerry.'

I was dumbfounded. Anne, apparently, was on a 24 hour stop-over in London, en route back to Africa from the United States. She asked me whether I was prepared to go on doing the fund-raising work, because she had heard how well my talks had been going.

'I don't see why not, Anne,' I replied. 'I seem to have made quite a good start.'

'Right,' she said, 'I want you to come back to Nairobi, bring a camera, stay with me as my guest, and I will ensure that you are shown much more of the work of the Flying Doctor Service.

Chapter Six

Across the Atlantic

When I returned home, laden with slides and souvenirs of my second trip to East Africa, I was confronted with absolutely masses of mail. My supporters at home had certainly not forgotten about me, and there were literally dozens of letters from all over the country - Womens' Institutes, Rotary Clubs and the like, requesting me to speak to their members. I was certainly going to be a busy lady!

One of the first things I did was to make some sort of effort to organise my work. I opened six files, one for Womens' Institutes and the others respectively for Townswomens' Guilds, Inner Wheels, Churches, Schools and miscellaneous organisations such as Ladies' Circles, Trefoil Guilds and so forth. The invitations were then placed in the appropriate files, and I was now able to set about the marathon task of sifting through all this paperwork so as to meet as many of these commitments as I possibly could.

There was another very interesting letter, and this I set about replying to as soon as ever possible.

Prior to my trip to Africa I had made friends, through my church, with some people who lived in Indiana, USA, in a place with the intriguing name of 'Rolling Prairie'. My good friend Varner Chance and his family were the leading lights behind the 'Sounds of Hope' choir, which tours around the world giving concerts of sacred music. In the past I had frequently played host to members of this choir when they had been performing at our church in Cheam and Varner had often expressed the hope that I might stay with them in Indiana.

When he heard that I was touring England giving talks about AMREF he was even more anxious that I should visit them, since they were all most interested to hear about my travels.

Among my many letters was one from Varner's daughter, Rebecca, inviting me to stay with her family in Indiana and to tell them all about AMREF and show them my slides. She also hoped to arrange for me to give a talk to her local church in Indiana. By this time I had, of course, caught the 'travel bug' with a vengeance, and I immediately wrote back accepting this invitation and arranged a travel date.

Of course, before I could leave for America there was a great deal of work to do in organising my talks, and before very long I was once again off in my little mini travelling the country.

One of the invitations which I received has led to a long and lovely friendship. It was from Valerie Mountford, the organiser of the 'Good Companions Club', a discussion group attached to the Crofton Baptist Church at Orpington, Kent. A speaking engagement had been unexpectedly cancelled, and Valerie was desperate for a replacement speaker. She was so delighted that I was able to 'step into the breach' that we have been close friends ever since.

Another interesting letter came from the 'Inner Wheel' at a town near Bury, Lancashire. I had already given a talk to a group in nearby Bury, prior to my second African trip, and had stayed as the guest of the organiser of this group. At least I .knew my way!

Not wishing to make the long haul to Bury all in one go I decided to stop off en route and stay overnight at a guest house. On such occasions I often used to like to play a little game with myself. Taking a road map, I would circle an area in the vicinity of my destination and stick a pin in the centre of this area. On this occasion my pin landed on Cannock, in Staffordshire. So I thought: 'If the Good Lord wants me to go to Cannock He must have a reason, so that's where I'll stay.'

And He did have a very good reason!

On arrival in Cannock I found a nice little guest house and booked a room. This was a Saturday evening, and immediately opposite the guest house was a small Methodist church. 'Very convenient,' I thought, 'for attending church on Sunday morning.'

On the following morning I duly went over to the service, after which I was introduced to the minister, who turned out to be The Reverend James. I was wearing my AMREF lapel badge. The minister had a short and polite chat with me as I was leaving the service. I explained that I was on my way to Bury, and why, and then he spotted my lapel badge.

'Oh,' he said, 'I recognise that. It's the Flying Doctor Service in East Africa, isn't it?'

'Yes,' I said. 'How come you recognise it?'

'Do you know Jimmy James?' he enquired.

'Do you mean our leprosy surgeon?' I asked. 'I should certainly think I do. I've been watching him operate at a bush hospital in Alupe! Why do you ask?'

'Well,' he exclaimed, 'isn't that strange. He's my brother!'

And that is one of the most amazing 'Godincidences' that I can ever remember. I sent the Reverend James a postcard on my next visit to Africa!

The following morning I drove to my destination near Bury, arriving at the venue in the evening.

When I arrived a familiar voice greeted me:

'Hello again, Christine.'

It was my friend from Bury, who had evidently been so impressed with my previous talk, some two years ago, that she had travelled to the other town to hear me again. So she invited me to stay with her again. Some people are gluttons for punishment!

My second series of talks seemed to be going very well indeed, and it was very useful to have my wonderful collection of slides this time. Visual aids of this kind can really bring a talk to life, and they made my job much easier. I also had a little Masai stool, a Masai necklace and a camel bell. I had really brought these back as souvenirs, but I thought they might make interesting talking points for my audiences. They did!

As soon as I could arrange a fortnight's break between engagements I was off on my travels again, this time to 'Rolling Prairie'. Another great adventure looming - but on arrival at Heathrow airport I found that I had run into problems.

The travel agents had omitted to tell me that I needed a visa for the United States. Apparently American citizens do not require a visa for the UK, but at the time the converse did not apply. So before I could travel I had to go all the way to the American Embassy in London to arrange a visa. In the meantime the 'plane had to be held for me, which did not make me very popular with my fellow passengers! Nor was I, for my part, best pleased with the travel agents!

However 'all's well that ends well' and you can imagine my relief when I was eventually handed my visa. 'Now,' I was informed, 'you have a visa for all time.'

Needless to say, I still have it, and I will always treasure it. I was even given a complimentary bottle of champagne on the flight, by way of compensation!

I was met at O'Hare airport, Chicago, by Rebecca and taken to her home where I received a very warm American welcome. I was amazed to discover that in addition to the planned talk to her local church Rebecca had arranged for me to give a number of other talks, to various organisations in Indiana. If I found this prospect somewhat daunting, her next statement fairly took my breath away!

'How do you feel about going on television?' she asked.

I had never appeared on television in my life, and I was not sure that I wanted to.

'I don't think I fancy that much,' I replied.

'Oh,' she said, 'that's a pity. It's all settled for next Monday morning.'

'What is?' I asked.

'Your appearance on Dorothy's Chat Show' came the reply! My talk to the local church went extremely well, and gave me a certain amount of confidence for the scheduled television appearance, but I must admit I still viewed this with some degree of consternation.

Monday morning dawned, and there was what my friend Rebecca called 'a pea-soup fog'. I would not have described it as such, but there was certainly a heavy 'scotch mist'. I doubt if Rebecca had ever really met a true pea-soup fog, but it was a misty drive to the television studio.

The studio was in Gary, Indiana - a fair drive from Rolling Prairie. Because of the weather conditions we were about three quarters of an hour late, but eventually we arrived and were escorted to a very large, dark room, where we were told to sit down. Rebecca's husband, Joe, was with us as were their three children; an exciting day out for the youngsters, as well. Somewhat to my surprise the children were allowed to wander around the studios at will. However, they behaved very well.

After a while a camera crew arrived. A lot of lights were switched on, and this revealed a little studio set in the corner, which was evidently 'Dorothy's nest'. The whole motif was yellow and gold; there was a golden sofa, a table with a lot of yellow flowers, and yellow wall paper. Dorothy herself had very blonde hair. She certainly matched the set!

After the initial introductions were over the cameras sprang into action, and we were 'live on air' - another 'first' for Christine! I sat down with Dorothy, who asked me a number of questions about my travels to Africa and my work with the flying doctors, which I answered to the best of my ability. I remember producing my little Masai stool, which was only about six inches high and therefore easy to handle in front of the cameras. I also displayed the necklace and the camel bell, and explained a little about the Masai way of life. It was quite a short interview, but it seemed to be well received.

In addition to the good publicity generated by the television appearance there was one particularly constructive sequel. Apparently a representative of the local nurses' association had been watching 'Dorothy's Chat Show,' and she had evidently been so impressed by what she saw that she telephoned me at Rebecca's home the following evening asking to speak to me. She told me that the nurses' association wanted to donate to AMREF some surplus surgical instruments if I could get them out to East Africa. I was, of course, delighted at this kind offer, and willingly agreed to collect the instruments and take them back to England and thence to Africa.

As will be seen, this led to one highly amusing encounter with the security staff at O'Hare airport on my return home, but more of that later.

In addition to the talk to Rebecca's church fellowship meeting - which, as I have said, was extremely well received - I gave a number of other talks in the area. Some were to small 'at home' groups, mainly Rebecca's personal friends, and some were to larger organisations. A number of telephone calls were received from people who had been at my initial talk at the church and wanted to know more about AMREF's work. I certainly did seem to be generating some very good publicity 'across the Atlantic,' and I must say I felt quite proud of myself!

One invitation in particular led to a very substantial donation to AMREF funds. This was from the local Rotary Club in Indiana (or its American equivalent) of which Varner Chance was a leading member. My presentation was extremely well attended by representatives of the local business comuunity, and I was proud to come away with a very substantial cheque to take back with me to our London office. This also led to a very complimentary article in the local newspaper.

On one occasion, at the end of a talk to one of the church groups, one of the church officials came up to thank me.

'I enjoyed your talk very much,' he said. 'But how come you talk so funny?'

Quick as a flash, his friend remarked:-

'She doesn't talk funny at all. It's you who hear funny!'

Altogether I gave about six talks over the course of my three weeks in Indiana, in addition to the television appearance. I thoroughly enjoyed my stay out there in the wilds of 'Rolling Prairie,' and felt somewhat reluctant to return home. I knew, however, that the mail would inevitably be piling up back in suburbia, and 'duty was calling'. So soon I found myself back at O'Hare airport, en route to Heathrow.

I had put the collection of surgical instruments in with my hand luggage, knowing that they would show up on the airport security scanning equipment and would have to be declared. When I came to put the luggage through the scanner I explained that my flight bag was full of surgical instruments. I had a letter from the nurses' association explaining why I was in possession of a quantity of syringes, callipers and similar items. There was a very large, somewhat intimidating lady at the security desk.

'We need to see some identification,' she barked.

'You're already holding my passport,' I replied. 'Isn't that sufficient?'

'Oh no,' she said. 'We need more identification than that. Haven't you anything with your photograph on it, such as a driving licence?'

I explained that in England we do not display our photographs on our driving licences, as they do in America. And then I had a brainwave.

'I do have this,' I said - and handed her my London Transport Senior Citizens' Bus Pass.

It worked like magic!

There were about four uniformed security guards, and my bus pass was passed from hand to hand, and caused tremendous excitement. They had never seen such a document - it could have been the Crown Jewels for all the interest it was generating!

'Just look at this lady's ID,' one cried out. 'Did you ever see such a goddamn thing in all your life?'

They never even examined the contents of the flight bag. The syringes could quite easily have been loaded with heroin and cocaine for all they cared - all they were interested in examining was one London Transport Senior Citizens' Bus Pass!

And that was how AMREF's headquarters in Nairobi subsequently came to be the proud possessors of a smart set of American surgical instruments. I delivered them personally on my next visit to Africa.

I returned home to be greeted by yet more piles of mail, and as soon as possible I got round to the task of filing and sorting my latest batch of invitations. One of these was totally unexpected, and led to a very interesting week in Cornwall.

This letter was from a lady whom I had met some years previously, whilst on holiday in Israel. She was a Methodist, and was helping to organise a big missionary rally at a large Methodist church in Redruth, Cornwall. This lady had heard of my work on behalf of the East African Flying Doctors. Representatives from various charities and missionary organisations were invited to set up stands in the church, displaying literature and information relating to their various organisations, and each representative was to be allocated an evening during the course of the week to give a presentation.

This promised to be an unique opportunity to undertake a week of 'fund-raising with a difference' and also to enjoy some good west country air, and so I accepted with enthusiasm.

On the appointed day I loaded up my little car with my projector, slides and display equipment and made my way to Redruth. We were each invited to stay at the homes of the various organisers. I stayed with a very pleasant, elderly lady and enjoyed an extremely worthwhile and interesting week.

Each day was spent at the church, where we all ate together. The whole affair was very well organised. The catering was provided by Mr. Rodda of the famous Rodda's Creamery and Turkey Farms in Cornwall, and so needless to say we were extremely well fed!

The week was certainly profitable for AMREF. On each day I left my AMREF collecting tin on my stand, with various leaflets and pictures relating to our work. Each evening I found the tin full of money. I certainly raised more funds in the course of this single week than I could have done in several separate speaking engagements. When it came to my evening to give a presentation this was extremely well received, and this provided me with an opportunity to 'spread the word' to an entirely different forum. I was even asked to give a short address from the pulpit. Never having regarded myself in any way as a 'preacher' or 'missionary' I found this a somewhat daunting prospect, but I think I acquitted myself reasonably well. It was a new experience, in any event.

Being a Methodist gathering, obviously most of the speakers and 'missionaries' were from Christian groups and organisations, and I certainly met and mixed with some extremely interesting people - some of them very well-known names indeed. Among these was Brother Andrew, who will be well-known to many readers through his famous book 'God's Smuggler' - the story of how Brother Andrew contrived - at tremendous personal risk - to 'smuggle' large quantities of bibles to countries behind the iron curtain in the days of the former Soviet Union. I was also privileged to meet Dr. Helen Roseveare, the well-known missionary doctor. All in all, it really was a most fascinating and profitable week - one of the most rewarding functions I have ever attended as a representative of AMREF.

After another full week away my speaking invitations were again piling up, and on my return I once again found myself with little spare time on my hands. I took the opportunity to fulfil various local commitments, among them a talk to the Trefoil Guild (a branch of the Girl Guides) at my local Methodist church in Cheam, and talks to a number of local church organisations. At about this time I was also invited to fulfil a very interesting and enjoyable speaking engagement to an 'Inner Wheel' meeting in Musselburgh, near Edinburgh, where I spent a very pleasant couple of days.

It was by now some time since I had visited our London office, and I still owed them a fistful of dollars which I had collected on my visit to Indiana. I therefore took the first available opportunity to visit Nicola Blundell-Brown in London.

By this time Nicola had opened files with the names and addresses of every secretary of every organisation to whom I had spoken. In view of the enormous number of speaking engagements I had fulfilled since I started this work this must have been quite a mammoth task in itself! However it was very gratifying indeed to know that the office was taking such a keen interest in my activities.

I also discovered that many of my talks had produced useful 'spin-offs' which were providing additional funds for AMREF. A surprising number of organisations, and in particular Womens' Institutes, were organising their own independent fund-raising activities for us, and in some cases were accepting AMREF as their 'Charity for the Year'. For this reason, I discovered, my efforts had given rise to additional income of which I had been totally unaware.

AMREF had by this time grown out of all proportion since my first visits to East Africa, and naturally it was important for me to continue to keep abreast of all developments in Nairobi. If my talks were to be kept up to date I would continuously need new material, new slides and new experiences to relate. A stale speaker can be in danger of becoming a boring speaker, and I therefore tried to ensure that I revisited East Africa every two years or so. There is little point in giving talks, and answering questions, unless you are absolutely sure of your facts.

Quite apart from these considerations, I was of course very keen to see all my friends in Nairobi as regularly as could possibly be managed, and to have as many chances as possible to stay at my new-found 'home from home,' the CPK guest house. Life would not seem the same without regular doses of Dinah and Nelson Kivuti and their staff!

In the late Spring of 1980, therefore, I found myself once again 'out in the bush' with Anne Spoerry, visiting bush hospitals in her little Piper Cherokee. This was again a very enjoyable and worthwhile trip, and I returned home armed with loads of new material to keep my talks alive and fresh. As I settled down at home to sift through my latest speaking invitations I must confess that I found myself feeling guiltily envious of Anne's ability to take off into the skies at will.

'She's sixty,' I thought to myself, 'if she's a day.' 'Suppose she had a heart attack, or something. You really ought to know how to land the thing' …

'Don't be silly, Christine,' I reproved myself. 'You know that's just an excuse' …

'If she can do it,' I replied, 'so can you' …

'You know perfectly well that you can't start learning to fly at the age of sixty-nine,' I replied. 'Do be your age' …

Or could I?

Perhaps I could try …

It would certainly be fun …

So I did!

Above: Self help ~ digging a well at Kanunguni. Below: AMREF Titan aircraft ready to transport manuals.

Above: The AMREF printing department. Below: The surgical team at work at Lodwar Hospital.

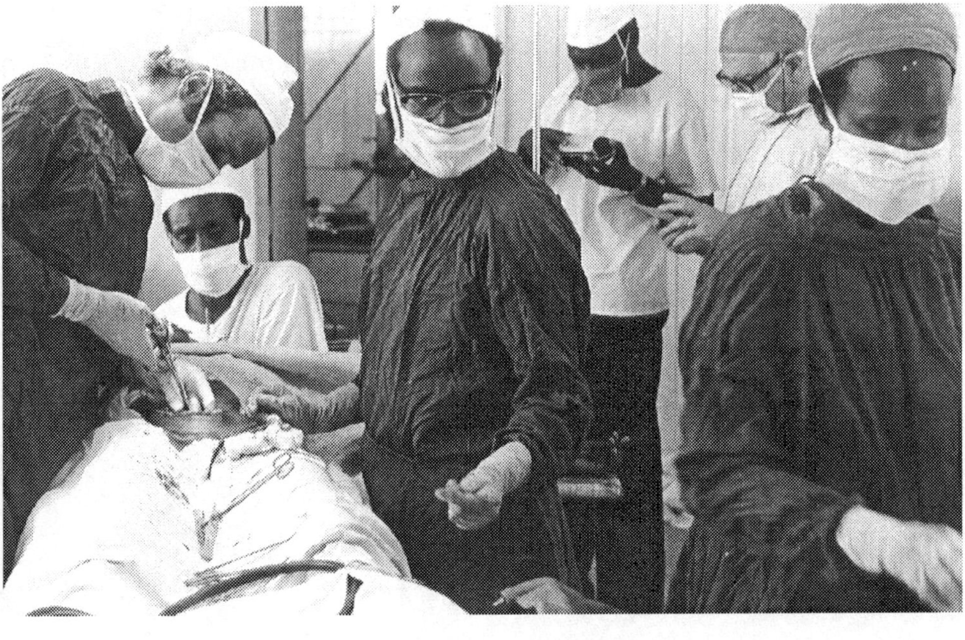

The author at home...

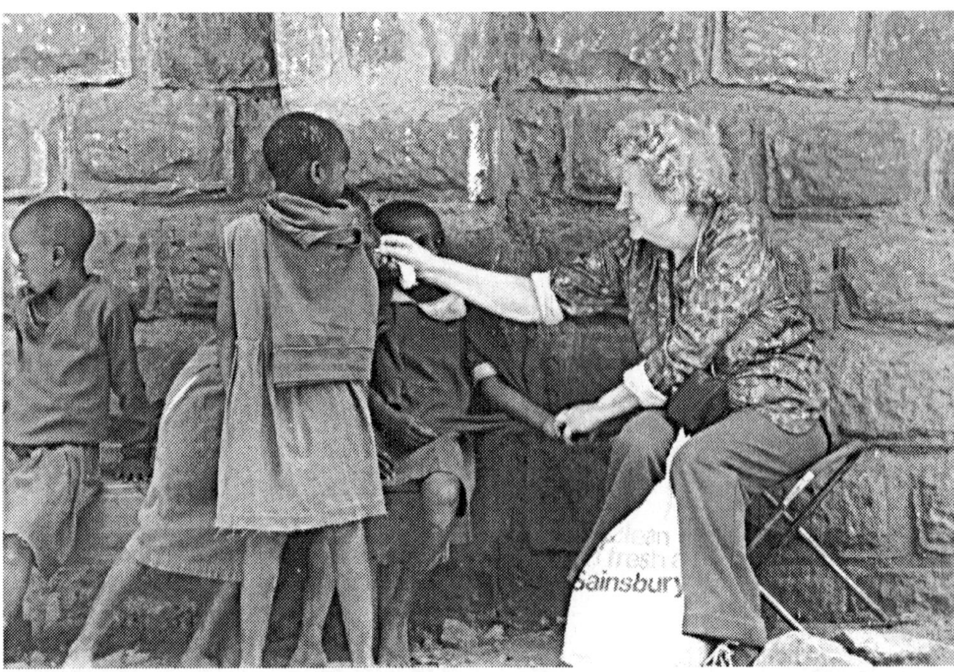

in the bush!

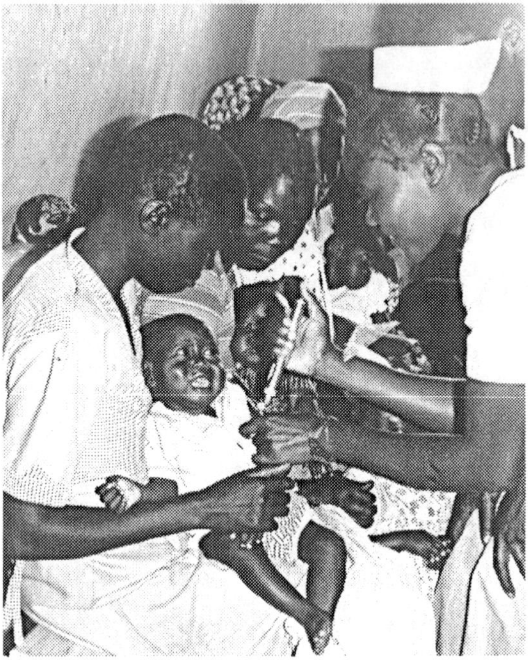

It won't hurt!

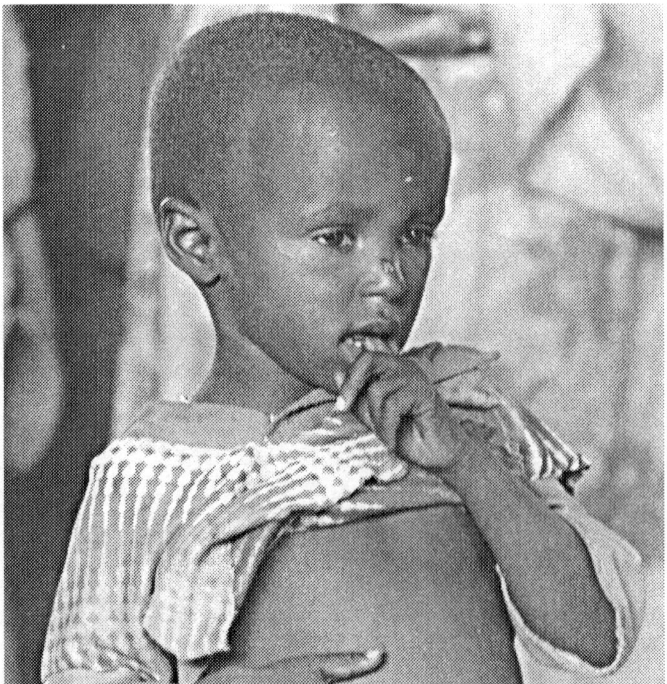

Above: The surgical team at Loitokitok: Below: The AMREF Mobile Unit.

Above: The AMREF Mobile Unit. Below: The author at Kimuka School with headmaster Maurice Douana.

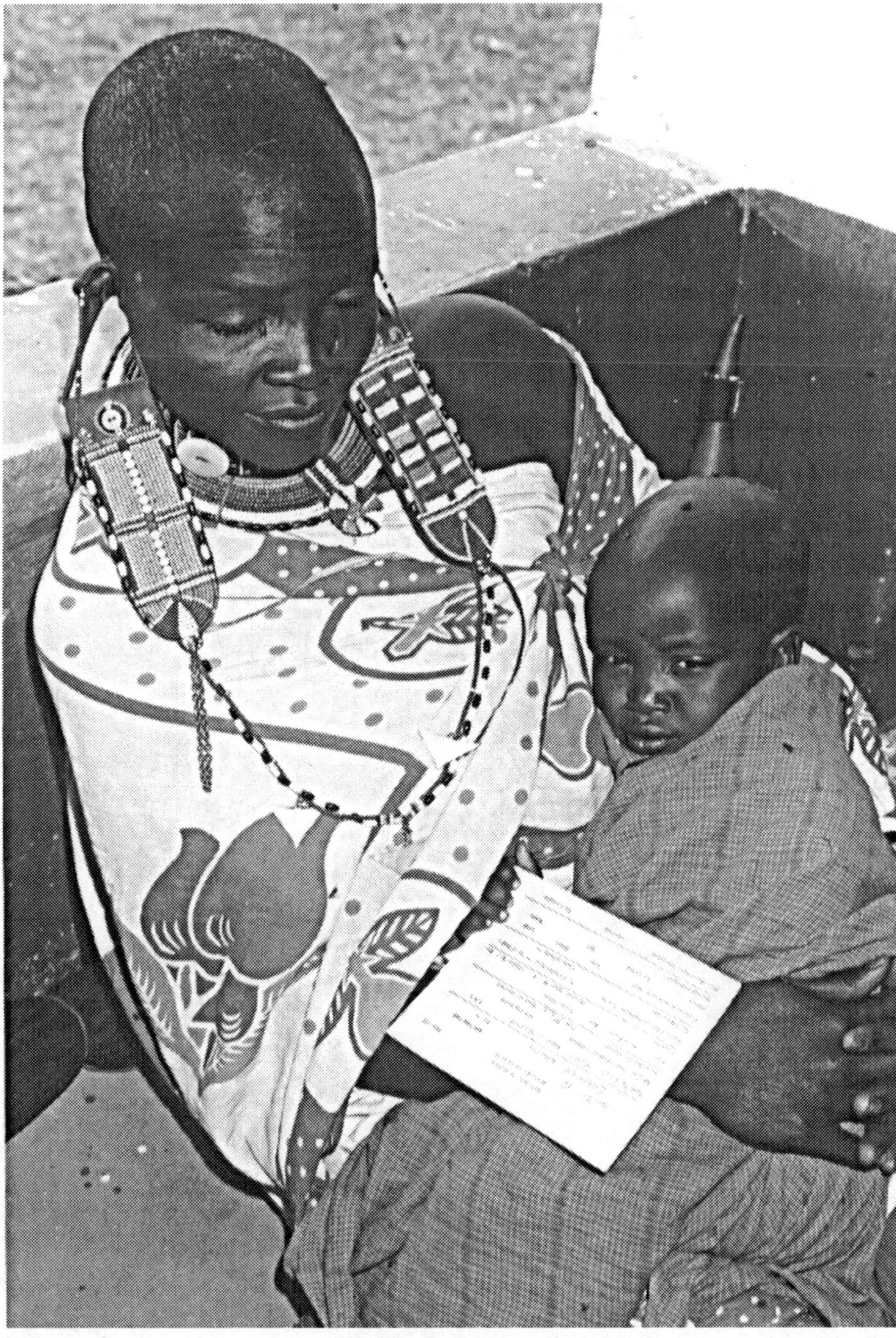

Patients awaiting treatment

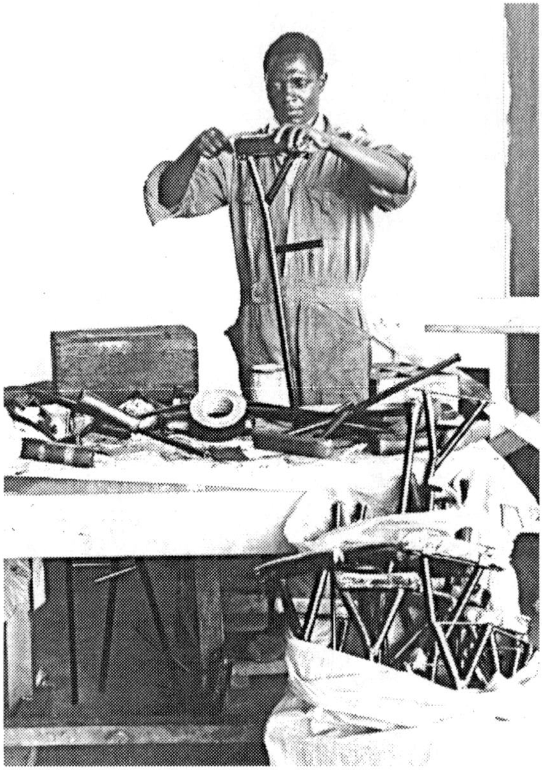

Above: The AMREF workshop. Below: Out into the bush.

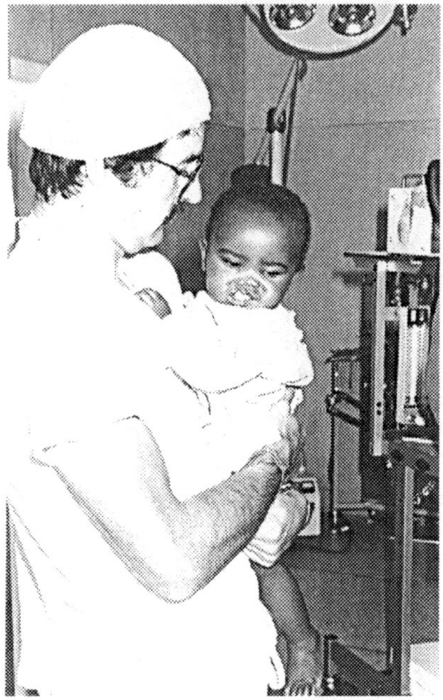

Above: Surgeon and child. Below: The work goes on!

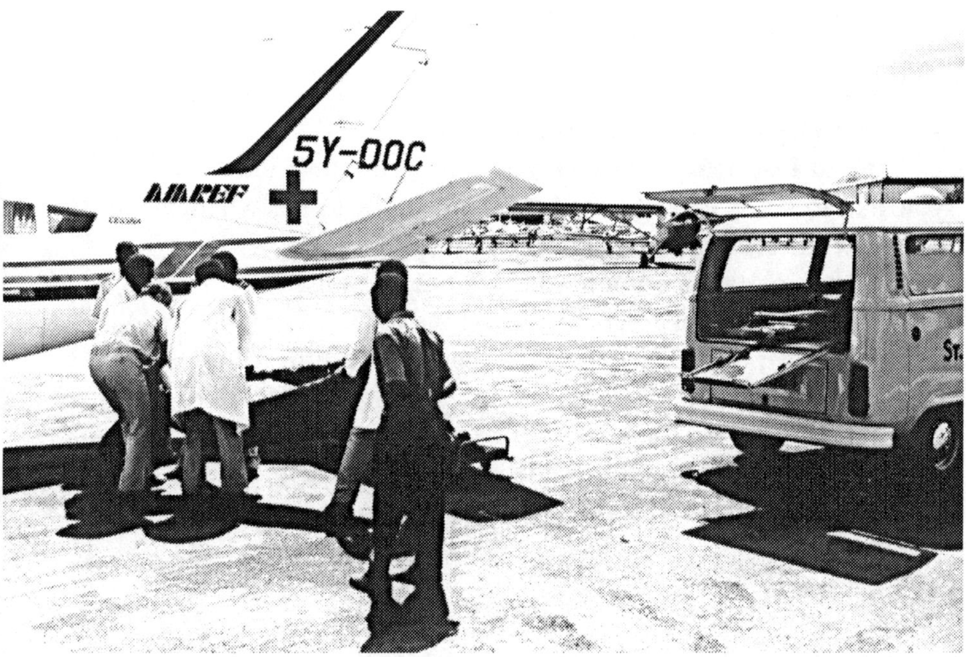

Chapter Seven

Flying High

Summer 1980. It was a glorious, beautiful sunny day. It was also a free day for me, clear of speaking engagements and other AMREF commitments. The housework was getting a bit neglected, but I thought to myself: 'Be blowed to housework. Its perfect flying weather. I'm going to see whether I can learn to fly.'

So out came the car, and off I went to Biggin Hill.

I walked into the first flying club I came to. Behind the counter was a very tall gentleman - well over six feet tall.

'Is there any age limit,' I asked, 'for learning to fly a 'plane?'

'No,' he replied, 'not so long as you pass the medical.'

'I am sixty-nine,' I said.

'That's all right,' he repeated, just so long as you pass the medical.'

He did not tell me how long the medical as going to take, or how much it was going to cost, but I was not in the mood to bother about such details. All I wanted to do was to get into an aeroplane and try to learn to fly it! And then he said:-

'I'm an instructor, and I've got a cancellation right now. Would you like to come up with me for a trial flight to see whether you're going to like it before you sign on?'

This was certainly an opportunity not to be missed.

'Oh, yes,' I said eagerly, 'I would love to.'

Out we went to the tarmac, and there was a little 'Beagle Pup', a small, dual controlled light aircraft, much smaller than a Piper Cherokee. There was just room for the pilot and one pupil. He took it up and flew it around for a short while. Then:

'You take control,' he said, 'and I'll tell you what to do.'

I must admit that I felt a bit scared. Not for the first time in recent years I wondered what I had taken on! However there was no going back now.

And so I took the controls, and we flew around for a bit. After a while I began to feel acclimatised, and by now I really was beginning to enjoy myself. The early nerves had passed away. 'This is the life,' I thought to myself. I asked a few questions about the controls, and they did not seem too complicated. I really did feel I was doing rather well. Then he said:

'You're looking too much at the instrument panel. I want you to steer by the horizon.'

'What horizon?' I asked. 'I can't see any horizon. I can only see out of the side window.'

As I have said, he was over six feet tall. And I'm a midget by comparison - barely five feet!

'What,' he said, sounding somewhat alarmed, 'can't you see over the instrument panel?'

'No,' I said. 'I can only see the instruments. I thought that was what you wanted me to do!'

He said, very bluntly, 'bring a couple of cushions next time!'

At least he was talking about a 'next time'. After flying around for half an hour with a pupil who could not see where she was going I would not have blamed him if he had given me up as a hopeless case. 'At least,' I thought to myself, 'he hasn't written me off altogether!'

The instructor, Ian, and I have subsequently become firm friends. We still keep in touch regularly. He has often told me that he has dined out on that story more than once - how he once gave a flying lesson to a pupil who couldn't see where she was going.

Despite this, I thoroughly enjoyed that first lesson. I drove back home happily - at least I could see through the windscreen of my little mini - and I decided that I would definitely go in for the medical and take a course of lessons.

The medical was carried out by a C.A.A. Doctor, and was quite rigorous. It involved a sight test, a hearing test and a general medical check-up. It was also, incidentally, quite expensive. However I was not going to let that put me off; nothing, now, was going to prevent me from learning to fly. By this time I had the bit well and truly between my teeth!

In point of fact, I was very reassured to know that medical tests for would-be pilots are so stringent. I sometimes wonder whether similar check-ups should be introduced for motorists. That might go some way towards reducing the appalling death toll on our roads.

In any event, I passed the medical without difficulty and went on to take a course of lessons. It was all a tremendous amount of fun. I got to know all the young flying instructors at the club very well, and I think I was something of a celebrity down there at the time, since I don't think they had ever had a pupil of my age before!

Over the course of the next year or so I think I had about forty flying lessons in all, and each one seemed more enjoyable than the last. Of course, there is much more to be learned than just mastering the controls of the 'plane. In the same way as a learner driver has to learn the highway code I had to do my 'homework' on meteorology, cloud formations, navigation and the like, and it was all quite hard work - but fascinating work as well.

All this was making me quite a debating point within my own family. At one stage a representative of the 'Evening Standard' contacted me; there had recently been a feature in a Womens' Magazine called *My Weekly* about my work for AMREF, and this had mentioned that I was taking flying lessons. The *Evening Standard* had got hold of this story and apparently considered that a paragraph about an elderly widow learning to fly would make amusing reading!

In any event a small paragraph came out in the *Evening Standard* under the caption 'Flying Grandmother'

This was seen by one of my grandsons, who proudly showed it to all his school-friends. Apparently he told them that his grannie was flying all over Kent on a beagle puppy! This must have conjured up a very interesting picture in the minds of his young audiences!

After that I was a very popular Grannie indeed. I remember my grandsons David and Graeme coming down on one occasion to the flying club. David, who is very keen on photography, took various photographs of me in front of the 'plane, and he compiled an album which he entitled 'Flying Grannie'. I believe that he has still kept this album to this day. I remember that the following summer I went on holiday to Gloucestershire with the boys and their parents, and they spent a lot of time asking me questions about cloud formations and meteorology. I can't guarantee that I gave them all the right answers, but I tried.

I made my first 'solo' flight after about twenty lessons, which is supposed to be quite good. By this time I was reasonably confident of my ability to get the 'plane up and down again without too much trouble - that, after all, was the whole object of the exercise originally. Ian, my regular instructor, was not at the club that day, which was a bit disappointing. I had been rather hoping to have a chance to 'show-off' to Ian. 'Never mind,' I thought to myself. 'Let's get on with it.'

I boarded the 'plane, took the controls, and within no time there I was, flying solo around the skies above Biggin Hill. I felt quite elated. 'Anne Spoerry,' I thought to myself, 'you're not the only senior citizen who can fly an aeroplane. Now you've got me to contend with!' But my confidence soon began to evaporate when I remembered that I had to face the prospect of landing the 'plane by myself for the first time. 'Come down to earth, Christine,' I told myself; 'Otherwise you may be forced to come down with a big bump!'

After flying around for the requisite period I levelled off, descended and, much to my relief, made a reasonably smooth landing on the runway. As I climbed out of the 'plane a familiar face greeted me.

'Congratulations, Captain Matthews!'

It was Ian, who unknown to me, had been at the club all the time. Perhaps he had not wanted to make me nervous.

I had made my first solo flight, and I must confess that I felt quite proud of myself.

After that I took about twenty more lessons, and each one made me a little more proficient. I went through the requisite training in what is called 'circuits and bumps', which involves taking off, making a circuit of the airfield, and landing again. I think I had to put in about ten hours of this in all.

I never went on to pursue a full licence. I didn't think this would really be worth my while. I did however obtain an emergency licence, which would have enabled me to land a light aircraft in an emergency, which was all I had really set out to do in the first place. At least this would have enabled me to land Anne's plane in the event of her having a heart attack in mid-air with me as passenger.

Thankfully, she never did.

And I'm quite sure she never will do.

As I said, this was only an excuse!

Chapter Eight

Golden Years

From my early years with AMREF one of our most illustrious supporters has been our Patron, HRH Prince Charles, the present Prince of Wales.

In the early nineteen 1980's AMREF held a cocktail party in honour of His Royal Highness in London, and I was highly honoured to be invited to attend this function. Little did I think, when I first tentatively went to see Nicola Blundell-Brown at the London office back in 1972, that within a few years I would be being introduced to Royalty as a representative of AMREF!

I was introduced to Prince Charles, and I duly curtsied to the best of my ability, feeling somewhat nervous and out of place, but His Royal Highness soon put me at my ease. I found him a charming man, and very easy to speak to. If I was a little unsure as to what to say following this introduction, uncertainty soon turned to hilarity.

'And are you a flying doctor?' enquired his Royal Highness.

'No,' I replied, 'just a keen voluntary supporter'

Eyeing the two tall Trustees who were acting as my escorts, he asked:

'And who are you married to?'

'Unfortunately,' I replied, 'nobody now, sir. I am a widow.'

To which one of the Trustees intervened:

'There you are, sir. She's free now!'

The Prince smiled and passed on to the next guest.

Although a recent article in my local newspaper has seen fit to refer to me under the caption 'African Queen' I have never had any aspirations to be Queen of England!

Not long after this incident a second opportunity to meet Prince Charles came my way. AMREF was allocated two tickets to a Buckingham Palace garden party. The foundation nominated me and a Mr. Winnington-Ingram, who had been involved with AMREF for a number of years, to represent them.

When I took my place in the line of guests awaiting presentation to Prince Charles I hoped very much that my appearance would not let me down. Shortly before this I had suffered a minor fall in my garden whilst hanging up the washing, and had a rather ugly bruise to my face. I had done my best to conceal this with a small veil, but nevertheless I was slightly apprehensive. All was well, however, and my presentation passed without adverse comment!

I remember being highly impressed, at this garden party, with Prince Charles's concern for the disabled. There were a number of guests in wheel chairs, and he made a point of visiting, individually, each and every disabled guest to shake hands before the tea commenced. I found this a very touching gesture.

1980 was to prove to be a busy year for me on the home front. Not very long after the garden party at Buckingham Palace I received a letter from the Legal & General Insurance Company, inviting me to telephone them. I did not have the remotest idea what this could all be about, and, intrigued to say the least, I duly telephoned the given number and was connected to the appropriate extension.

'Ah, yes, Mrs. Matthews,' came a voice. 'I am pleased to tell you that you have reached the London Area Finals of our Golden Years Competition.'

I hadn't the faintest idea what this could all be about.

'I don't understand,' I said. 'How can I possibly have reached the finals of a competition which I haven't even entered?'

'Oh, somebody must have nominated you,' I was informed.

It transpired that my eldest grandson, David, had seen details in the *TV Times* of a competition to find the 'Liveliest Senior Citizen' in Britain. Having so recently been watching his grandmother flying circuits around Biggin Hill he had evidently taken it upon himself, quite unbeknown to me, to put my name forward for this prestigious title! It appears that this contest was to provide publicity for a television 'sitcom' called 'Young at Heart' starring John Mills which, as some readers may possibly remember, was all about energetic pensioners. Apparently David had given them a lot of information about my work for AMREF and my flying lessons, and they had spent many days sorting through the thousands of entries before compiling a short-list of six finalists for the London area, of which I was one.

Soon afterwards I received a formal letter confirming my selection, and inviting me to stay overnight at the Kensington Court Hotel in London where the adjudication was to be held. I was invited to bring a friend or relative as my guest, and all this was to be at the expense of the Legal & General Insurance Company. This promised to be a most unusual and exciting occasion, and I was very much looking forward to it.

On the appointed day my son and I duly arrived at the hotel and were conducted to our rooms. There was an enormous bowl of flowers in my room, all provided by the organisers, and a little note welcoming me to the function and congratulating me on my success to date. I was told to present myself in the hotel lounge the following morning, when I would meet the other contestants and where the judges would be making their decision. 'Win or lose,' I thought to myself, 'I'm certainly being well looked after!'

On the following morning I was introduced to the other five finalists. We were certainly an assorted bunch. The only thing we all had in common, apart from being elderly, was that each of us was involved, in some way, in voluntary work for others. One lady made toys for distribution to deprived children in the East End of London; there was a Battle of Britain fighter pilot who had suffered severe burns when shot down, and who was one of Sir Archibald

McIndoe's original 'Guinea Pigs'; the other finalists included a severely disabled lady who made artificial flowers to raise funds for handicapped children. It was certainly interesting to meet and talk to these people from such different backgrounds - all of whom had, like me, been nominated by devoted friends and relatives.

During the course of the morning we were all plied with coffee and cocktails, and at intervals we were called in, one by one, to the interview room. When my turn came I discovered that the adjudication panel consisted of the Mayor of Kensington, a representative of the Legal & General, one of the production staff of the television programme and various other local dignitaries. I was asked various questions about my work for AMREF and the reasons for my involvement, all of which I answered to the best of my ability. 'At least,' I thought to myself, 'this is another opportunity to 'spread the word' even if I do not get anywhere!'

In the evening there was a big dinner. The six contestants and their guests all sat at one table, which gave us a further opportunity to share our experiences whilst awaiting the 'big decision'. I was seated next to the burned fighter pilot, and he was of particular interest to me in view of Sir Archibald McIndoe's early association with Michael Wood when the East African Flying Doctor Service was in its infancy. This gentleman was heavily involved with charitable work for other 'Guinea Pigs', and I found him most impressive.

At the end of the dinner the Mayor rose to his feet and announced the judges' decision. As always seems to be the case in these competitions the successful candidates were announced in reverse order, which made us all feel rather like something out of a 'Miss World' contest. Eventually I heard my name being called out.

'And now, the runner-up. Mrs. Christine Matthews.'

I went forward to receive my award - a beautiful glass paperweight containing a colourful model sea-anemone and bearing the legend 'Legal & General Golden Years Award 1980' - and was duly congratulated by the Mayor. The winner was the lady who made toys for the East End children; I was disappointed to note that my friend from the Guinea Pigs was not in the placings.

This was another thoroughly enjoyable occasion, and once again I had good cause to thank God for placing that wonderful library book in my hands and for prompting me so strongly to follow it up by contacting AMREF. I had now spent eight richly rewarding years, made four trips out to Africa, learned to fly, made some beautiful new friendships and had now received this thoroughly unexpected award. I felt the luckiest lady alive!

Those were indeed my 'Golden Years', those early years in the 1980s. My lecture tours had now settled down into an ordered pattern, and these continued to raise much-needed funds for AMREF. By this time the problems of poverty in Africa were regularly featured on UK news bulletins - this was the time of the famines in Ethiopia and Biafra, and people were therefore becoming much more conscious of the problems of the developing countries. I have no doubt that this produced a considerable 'spin-off' effect insofar as my own talks were concerned.

I continued to visit East Africa every two years or so, partly to keep abreast of new developments and to keep my material up to date and also to see as much as possible of all my friends in Nairobi. They were also very busy years on the home front, and very few weeks passed without my little mini and me being seen exploring the leafy lanes of Britain. I was certainly a busy lady - and a very happy one.

'This can't last for ever,' I sometimes thought to myself. 'I suppose I'll have to slow down some day...

...But certainly not yet!'

Chapter Nine

Back To The Bush

1986 - fourteen years from the date of my first, tentative steps in East Africa, and now once again I was winging my way back to the bush. It was now two years since my previous fact-finding visit, which had been in 1984, many waters had passed under the bridge, and once again I was in need of new material.

I was also very much in need of another dose of Dinah and Nelson Kivuti and all my friends at the CPK guest house, and after clearing through customs at Nairobi I made a bee-line for my 'home from home'.

I received my usual warm welcome from Dinah and Nelson, Charles, my room boy, Ruth and Naomi on the front desk and all my other friends. By this time I really was treated as an important part of this big, warm happy family. There was also a lovely bowl of flowers from Stephen, my AMREF driver who looked after me so well throughout this visit.

One of my hobbies is fine embroidery, and I had made for Dinah and Nelson a large embroidered picture, and had framed this for them. It was an Autumn garden scene, with a picture of a bird on a tree, and I had thought that a little bit of England on their wall might be of interest to the staff and guests.

Dinah was delighted with this gift, and said that she wanted to have it in her office. The office is just inside the front door, and can be seen from the hall through a glass window.

'I want it on that wall over there,' she said, pointing through the window into the office, 'so that everybody can see it as they come in.'

She seemed to be pointing directly at a portrait of President Moi of Kenya.

'Oh,' she exclaimed with disappointment, 'we can't have it there, can we! We have to have him, don't we?'

In Kenya it is almost mandatory to display a prominent portrait of the revered president, just as it used to be the custom for British homes to display a portrait of the royal family on the living room wall.

But Dinah was really keen to display my embroidery in the space occupied by President Moi, and seemed really disappointed that this did not seem possible. 'Surely you can put it on the opposite wall,' I suggested.

'No,' she insisted, I don't want it on the other wall - I want it there, where it can be seen as soon as anybody comes in. It's so beautiful.'

I was highly flattered, but I did not want my gift to be the subject of a diplomatic incident!

Eventually she said: 'It's no good; I'm not having it on any other wall. I'll just have to move the President along a little bit. I'm sure he won't mind, and if he does it's just too bad!'

So my embroidered picture was moved to the centre of this wall, and President Moi was relegated to a less prominent position. Some years later I attended a big dinner at AMREF headquarters, and President Moi was the guest of honour. I was introduced to him, and I told him how he had been moved along the wall of the guest house to make room for my embroidery. He thought it was a huge joke!

Dinah and Nelson insisted that at some stage in the course of this visit I must find time to visit their own home in Embu and to stay with them as their guest. This was a lovely invitation, and one which I was determined to accept. However, there was work to be done, and I promised that just as soon as I could make time I would spend a long weekend with them in Embu.

The following morning I went, by appointment, to AMREF headquarters at Wilson airport, where I was met by Anne Spoerry. Anne had by that time moved from her previous home in Subukia, and was now living at Lamu, an island in the Indian Ocean just off the east coast of Kenya. She invited me to spend a few days at her new home later on during my visit. Invitations seemed to be coming to me thick and fast, and this was something else to look forward to.

But now, as I have said, it was time for work. By this time I was very well-known to many of the staff at AMREF headquarters - Daniel, our blind telephonist, Danieli, who is a driver with the mobile unit, and many others. These included my very good friends Robbie and Rosemary, two English V.S.O. nurses who went out to Kenya many years ago and with whom I had made many journeys out into the bush.

I was delighted to see all these good friends again and to hear all the latest AMREF news and adventures. Danieli, particularly, had recently had the most hair-raising experience which he recounted to me. Apparently they had been camping in the Kenyan bush when a herd of elephants decided to migrate through the camp. Danieli got into his van and drove round and round the camp, blowing his horn and creating as much noise as he could in order to disperse these elephants. Much as I like adventure I must confess to having been rather glad not to have been present on this particular occasion!

Robbie and Rosemary invited me to accompany them in their car on a famine relief trip. Famine Relief, though not technically the specific responsibility of AMREF, is nevertheless, of course, a very important aspect of third world medical treatment and I was most interested to be invited on this trip.

I duly set off with Robbie and Rosemary, followed by several other vehicles manned mainly by volunteers, many of them young students who came to help serve the food. On the way, when we paused for a break in the journey, I noticed one gentleman, a minister, leaning up against his car with a spade in his hands. I asked him, somewhat flippantly, whether he was anticipating digging graves.

'No,' he replied, 'but I am anticipating getting my vehicle really bogged down in the sand!'

Our destination was a bush settlement, not very far from Nairobi. We arrived just about at the same time as the food lorry. People queue up at these lorries for their food tickets, which are distributed in accordance with the size of the family concerned and their general nutritional requirements. The food normally consists of the appropriate quantities of water, maize, oil, dried milk - the basic essentials.

While the adults were waiting in the queue I was asked to help look after the children and keep them out of mischief. I particularly remember one little boy, who I really thought I might end up having to bring back to England, so attached did he become to me.

He was about five years old, and was so emaciated that his legs and arms were like matchsticks. He was very unsteady on his feet, and was terrifically debilitated. However, he obviously had some strength left in his arms, because he clung to me like a limpet. He just would not move. Twice I took him back to Robbie and Rosemary, who said that they had been unable to trace his parents. Nobody seemed to know to whom he belonged, or anything about him. I don't know what happened to him in the end - something must have been done with this little waif.

I spent most of the rest of that day at this settlement, and I found it all very revealing and rewarding. Many people in our affluent western culture have little conception of the extent of hunger and poverty in these developing countries, and it can be a thought-provoking exercise to see it at first hand. It certainly was for me.

When I returned to the guest house there was a message asking me to be at the AMREF headquarters first thing the following morning. When I arrived I was met by Anne Spoerry, who invited me to accompany her to Lake Turkana, in northern Kenya near to the Ethiopian border, which is the home of the Gabbra and Turkana tribes and where Anne was due to visit various local AMREF field hospitals and clinics. We gave a lift to a local Oxfam representative, who had to check up on one of Oxfam's local fishing projects at the Oasis fishing camp at Loiangalani, on the east shore of Lake Turkana.

We landed at the airstrip at North Horr, which is not far from the east coast of the lake. However this did not prove to be a very easy exercise.

Just as we were due to level out and land a very heavy wind started to rock our small 'plane, and this whipped up all the sand around the airstrip. The consequence was that we found ourselves having to land in a sandstorm. We were almost flying blind - when you are in a sandstorm it is virtually impossible to see anything. How Anne Spoerry ever managed to land that 'plane I just do not know. Readers will recall that I had once had my own experience of 'flying blind', but in my case this was quite voluntary, there was no sandstorm at that time over Biggin Hill, and I had an instructor with dual controls! It is a great tribute to Anne's ability as a pilot that we managed to land at all.

When we finally did land it was as dark as pitch, and everything was totally clogged up with sand. I would not have liked to have been the mechanic who had to clean up and service that 'plane!

Whilst Anne visited her clinics I accompanied the Oxfam representative to Loiangalani. Oxfam is responsible for the supply of a number of the fishing boats at the Oasis fishing camp, and it was his job to check on the condition of these boats and to ensure that these were all complete and in good order. However one of the boats appeared to be missing and it took the man nearly all day to locate it. This did not bother me at all, since I was able to spend a lovely day relaxing by the lake. I don't, however, suppose that it was so much fun for the poor man who had to spend the entire day searching for one of his fishing boats. It turned out that one of the fishermen had carried off this boat to another nearby lake where he hoped that the fishing might be better!

This exercise was of interest to me for quite another reason. During my spare time at home one of my occupations is working as a voluntary helper at our local Oxfam shop in Cheam. It was therefore very interesting for me to see one of their projects in action, and I was able to recount this story to my fellow workers at the Oxfam shop when I returned home.

In the evening I travelled back with the Oxfam representative to North Horr, where we were met by Anne and flown back to AMREF headquarters at Wilson airport. The Oxfam man had left his car at the airport. I was still covered with sand from the storm.

'I'd better drive you back to your hotel,' he said bluntly after we had landed. 'You look as if you could do with a jolly good bath!'

I certainly was in need of a bath, and I thought this a good example of plain speaking at its best.

Shortly after this I was sent by AMREF on a trip to a childrens' home at Kajiado, which lies some eighty kilometres south of Nairobi. This was a particularly interesting experience.

This home is run by Sister Georgie Orme, an American lady, and specialises in the care and rehabilitation of children struck by poleomyelitis and other crippling bone diseases. The home combines normal schooling with medical treatment, and what I found of particular interest was a workshop on the premises specialising in the manufacture of callipers and other aids for the disabled children. This had been largely funded by AMREF and run by Daniel Sapoya, a local lad and former shoemaker who had been sent out to Germany to learn his craft. I was fascinated to watch Daniel at work, and the quality of his craftsmanship seemed to my inexperienced eye to be very high indeed. His little workshop was very well equipped with all the appropriate machinery, and I was touched by his concern for, and work on behalf of, these unfortunate children.

After a few more days visiting local clinics and helping out at AMREF headquarters it was time for me to enjoy my few days break with Anne Spoerry at her new home in Lamu. I had been very much looking forward to my mini-holiday on this island in the Indian Ocean. It all sounded most exciting.

From Wilson airport we flew down to an airstrip on the coast, from where we boarded a ferry to Lamu. Anne has a lovely house on the island, and when I was shown to my bedroom I found, to my delight, that there was an absolutely glorious view from the balcony over the Indian Ocean. There was a mass of bougainvillea by the balcony, and it really was a picture.

I was not the only house-guest. Anne also had a friend staying with her at the time and I spent a very pleasant long weekend with them. I remember buying a woven cloth at a local sale, and this gave me the good opportunity for a lovely swim in the Indian Ocean. Anne advised me that if I soaked the cloth in the ocean the salt would help to fix the colours. This seemed to me like a perfect excuse for a swim!

On my last day Anne sent me and her other guest down to the local shops to buy greengrocery. We came back with paper carrier-bags loaded up with the local produce which I emptied by hand and put away. This was, although I was not to know it at the time, to lead to problems. Later I wished that I had been wearing gloves.

When I woke up the next morning my hand had swollen up like a tennis ball, and was very, very painful. I showed my hand to Anne.

'My goodness,' she exclaimed, 'that is a poisonous spider bite.'

She advised me to keep the hand bathed with cold water and seek further advice when I returned to Nairobi that afternoon. When I returned to the guest house that evening I showed my hand to one of the guests who happened to be a doctor. He advised me to soak a towel in cold water, wrap it up tightly and keep the hand elevated above my head throughout the night. I found this rather difficult and uncomfortable, and I had a rather sleepless night. By the morning the bed was soaking wet from the towel, but at least the swelling had subsided. It took about three days to return to normal. This is an object lesson - never handle unwashed greengroceries in Africa without wearing protective gloves!

Very shortly after this it was time for me to take advantage of my other holiday invitation - this time as the guest of Dinah and Nelson Kivuti at their home in Embu.

Embu is a small town due north-east of Nairobi, and I stayed here with Dinah and Nelson for nearly a week, being very well looked after. Nelson is a governor of a school in that area, and he had recently heard that his school had won an award for being the best school in the district. Naturally he was very proud of this, and we went to visit the school to congratulate the children. African children always give a cheerful and warm welcome to foreign visitors, and this was no exception. However, on this occasion I did not succeed in providing them with any special English rain!

On the Sunday of my stay we went to their church in Embu. This was a very big church. Unlike most English churches, Christian churches in Kenya are very well attended; you almost have to queue to get in! I found this very encouraging indeed, and it says a lot about the spread of Christianity in the developing world.

In the middle of the service Dinah beckoned me up to the front.

'The Priest wishes to talk to you,' she said. 'Would you go up to the altar?'

So up I went to the Priest, with Dinah. He asked me a number of questions, my answers to which were duly translated to the congregation. I seemed to be quite a V.I.P.! I wished I could speak Swahili, but unfortunately I was never able to learn more than a few words of the language. However, I was able to take this opportunity to tell the congregation something of the work of AMREF and of my reasons for being in Kenya. It was certainly the first time I had heard my own testimony being delivered in a language which I myself couldn't understand, and it was quite a novel experience. My previous testimony in similar circumstances had, of course, been in Redruth, but there I had at least been able to deliver it personally!

After the service a gentleman from the congregation invited several of us to his home for lunch. He had recently been married, and he wished to celebrate this with us. We had a most enormous picnic lunch in his garden. I remember chickens running wild all over the garden. It was a lovely afternoon.

I was informed that the following day, Monday, was to be the Annual General Meeting of the Church Womens' Fellowship, and we were all invited to attend. I had, of course addressed hundreds of Church Womens' Fellowship meetings at home, speaking about the work of AMREF, but this was the first time I had ever taken part in a question and answer session with all the dialogue having to be translated into Swahili!

It was an altogether wonderful time, these few days in Embu, and I would have loved to stay longer. However, again my AMREF commitments were piling up - both in Nairobi and - of course - back at home. On more than one occasion I had cause to wonder what my post-bag was going to look like when I eventually returned home. So very shortly it was time to bid farewell to my new friends in Embu and to accompany Dinah and Nelson on the drive back to Nairobi.

After my return from Embu I spent a few days in Nairobi at AMREF headquarters at the airport, generally helping out, updating my information and trying to make myself useful. I did not travel very far afield during this short period since I was conserving my energies for what was to turn out to be my final 'East African Safari'.

It was now some fourteen years since my tour of the Ugandan game parks, when I had been mistaken for a hippopotamus at Paraa. I was by now seventy-five years old, and I suspected that this might be my last opportunity to 'go on safari'. (As it turned out my guess was correct).

I therefore arranged to join a party from Nairobi, visiting several game parks. This tour, also, was organised by Nile Star. We travelled from Nairobi down to the Manyara and Serengeti National Parks, the Ngorongoro Crater and returned to Nairobi by way of Treetops. One of our party was a Hungarian lady and most of the others were American. This was another opportunity to see some wonderful wildlife - many lions, giraffes and, of course, more of the beautiful East African birds.

The luxuriant Manyara National Park is one of the few such parks actually within the boundaries of the East African Rift Valley. Bordered on the east by the alkaline waters of Lake Manyara, the park runs on its western side up into the Manyara escarpment. This tree covered, often nearly vertical slope plunges down to the shores of the lake. The forest land of the park is a paradise of animals, birds and trees. Here we saw hosts of lions, baboons, blue Sykes monkeys and, of course, elephants. There is a bewitching variety of trees, and of particular interest to us were the enormous *Adansonia digitat*, or baobab trees. Several African tribes believe that the baobab is the home of night spirits. One legend has it that God was angry with the tree. It seemed to God to be the wrong way up and so he replanted it upside down. Its trunk is bulbous, and its branches certainly do have an upside down look. Baobabs are soft tissued, fleshy and frequently full of holes excavated by birds and small mammals. At night they are often visited by bats, and big eyed bush-babies creep around their branches in the dusk. It is therefore small wonder that these great trees have come to be associated with night spirits!

As is the case throughout East Africa the forest abounds with Acacia tortilis, the lovely flat-topped thorn trees so beloved of the elephant population. The elephants are often said to be destroying their habitat by ripping down these trees wholesale so as to get at their yellow seed pods. However, here there is an interesting and little known quirk of nature. Apparently if these seeds merely drop to the ground from the trees they are unlikely to germinate. If, however, they first pass through the elephant's digestive system they are much more likely to bear fruit. It seems that this has something to do with the action of the acid in the elephant's intestines. Whatever the cause, the maligned elephant seems, after all, to be helping to replace that which he consumes!

We travelled from Manyara to the vast Ngorongoro crater, and had our evening meal on a balcony overlooking the crater. This was a wonderful sight. There were lions, jackals, hyenas, many giraffes, many herds of wildebeest and every kind of deer imaginable. The whole place was absolutely teeming with wildlife.

Our evening meal at the Ngorongoro Crater was not quite such a success. It consisted of stewed impala, served with bananas and radishes. I found impala very indigestible, and it really made me quite ill. I do not recommend this particular dish to prospective safari makers.

After spending the night at Ngorongoro we proceeded to the famous Serengeti National Park. This, perhaps the most well-known of all the great East African National Parks, gave us still further opportunities to wonder at the mass of wildlife. Those who have never visited these areas should not imagine them as 'parks' in the traditional sense of the word. They are not enclosed spaces, although one does have to pass through a security gate before entering the area. Rather, they are enormous wildlife conservation areas, where the animals can roam at will with the minimum risk of being hunted or harmed.

The Serengeti is, of course, renowned for its proliferation of lions. One of the American couples had a son named Bobbie. Whilst we were in the Serengeti we saw so many lions that Bobbie said he was not going to take any more photographs of lions unless he saw a lion with two tails, and this became quite a standing joke on the trip - Bobbie's lion with two tails!

One day we were driving along the track when another game park van came hooting alongside us, their driver gesticulating to our driver to indicate that he had seen something of particular interest. We turned back and came to a clearing. Here there was an enormous tree, its branches spread out wide. We drove right up underneath this tree, and there were seven lions spread across the branches - two lionesses and five cubs. This was quite a sight to behold; I have since been told that it is only in the Serengeti that the lions normally climb the trees. Two of the cubs were lying tail to tail, with their tails hanging over one side of the tree. The way they were lying made it look exactly as if both these tails belonged to the same lion cub!

'Bobbie,' we cried, 'there's your lion with two tails!'

And so Bobbie did get his photograph after all!

After a night at the Serengeti we travelled on to Treetops, which lies due north of Nairobi. Our drive took us past Lake Magadi, which as it may be remembered had impressed me so much by its enormous display of flamingos when I had overflown the lake with Michael Wood back in 1974. Here I was able to learn more about the extraordinary phenomenon of these great soda lakes along the East African Rift Valley, and the reason behind their tremendous concentration of the beautiful pink flamingos.

These lakes are, in fact, little more than vast sumps of water and soda. This soda is sucked up from the thermal base of the Rift, and the sodaic content of the water, particularly in Lake Magadi and its neighbour to the south, Lake Natron, make the water rich in algae. The algae, together with the small, shrimp-like animals and tiny snails which are almost the sole inhabitants of these inhospitable waters, provide a valuable source of food for the flamingos, whose beaks have been adapted by nature so as to enable the birds to sift the food from the unpalatable water. It is for this reason that the soda lakes are such a haunt for Africa's three million flame-pink flamingos. They certainly cut an impressive picture against the sodaic pallor of the lake.

The food supplies in the soda lakes also provide an interesting explanation for the pink colouration of the flamingos. They contain canthaxanthin, a chemical substance similar to vitamin A, and this turns the flamingos pink. Away from the lakes they turn white. Apparently the reason why pink flamingos are seen in zoos is that they are fed synthetic canthaxanthin, so as to appease the public's expectation of pink flamingos!

During the evening we sat on the balcony watching the animals coming to the famous Treetops water hole.

Until that time I had never realised that elephants 'kiss'. However, during the evening along came two elephants, and I think they must have been very much in love! They kept fondling each other with their trunks, winding them around each others' necks. They then put their mouths together and it looked for all the world as if they were kissing each other. They had what looked like a really amorous session - it was like a romantic movie, especially staged for our benefit. It was all most touching!

There were also many hippopotami, several deer and giraffes, and one solitary young rhinoceros, who had apparently left his family and wandered off alone for his evening drink. We also saw many large families of baboons, and here we learned another valuable object lesson.

Anybody visiting Treetops would be very well advised never to leave their window open, even by the smallest crack. If they do they will soon find that the baboons will have robbed them of all their possessions! These thieving little devils have a nasty habit of putting their hands through any crack in the window and lifting anything in sight - wallets, handbags, jewellery, anything. The burglary rate is nearly as bad as it is in the suburbs of London!

The following morning we drove back to Nairobi, and I returned relaxed and refreshed, having experienced some wonderful new sights and sounds to relate to my friends and audiences on my return to England. Very shortly thereafter it was once again time to return home, and so after bidding my fond if reluctant farewells to Anne Spoerry and the AMREF staff - and, of course, my dear friends Dinah and Nelson and their staff - I made my way to Kenyatta Airport and thence back home.

This had been yet another really worthwhile trip, but I wondered very much, on that flight home in 1986, whether it might prove to be my last. At the age of seventy-five, I thought to myself, perhaps it might be sensible to think about taking life a little more easily; perhaps the time was approaching when I might have to give up all this globe-trotting and concentrate on my full time job of fund raising at home…

I wondered, sleepily, what the post would be like when I got home. Soon, I supposed, I would be on yet another round of speaking engagements…

How long would I be able to keep all this up?

Not for ever, surely!

For the first time ever on an aeroplane I slept.

Chapter Ten

Doorway To Health

I did manage to wake up before we landed at Heathrow, and wearily I made my way through the airport check-outs to the arrivals lounge, where I had arranged to be collected by a local taxi firm. This particular firm had, by now, become used to taking me to, and collecting me from, Heathrow and Gatwick airports and I had therefore become quite friendly with most of their drivers.

'Hello again, Mrs. Matthews. And where have you been this time?'

It is always a tonic for me to tell anybody who is prepared to listen about my travel experiences, and I chatted happily to the driver as we travelled the short distance from Heathrow to Cheam. I told him all about my latest experiences 'in the bush' and by the time I got home I was really feeling quite refreshed.

I had been right in my forecast that there would be a heavy post awaiting me. When I opened to door I was met by a whole mountain of mail. However it was by now too late to start work and so I decided to leave sorting all this out until the morning. 'Tomorrow's another day,' I thought to myself, 'and anyway, Christine, you know quite well that you can't possibly accept all these invitations. Remember what you decided on the aeroplane? You're just going to have to cut it down a bit.'

The following morning, after a good night's sleep, I set about the task of opening my mail and deciding how I was going to set about planning my work over the next few months... or years?

As anticipated, the invitations were from all over the country. Many of them were for repeat bookings from organisations to which

I had spoken over the past fourteen years. I knew that I could not possibly accept them all, and so I decided to sort them out into some sort of order of priority.

First of all I sorted the invitations into geographical locations. Those which were in the South of England, and therefore relatively local to me, were given priority. Those which were invitations to speak again at organisations who had already heard my talks came next; I feel that if people are so interested in hearing more about a subject upon which one has already spoken then they deserve to be accommodated. Finally, invitations which I could see no possible way of meeting were put on the third pile, and I set about the task of writing my reluctant letters of apology.

There was by that time another reason for not wishing to venture too far afield from home. Although I was still driving my car this was becoming increasingly difficult, particularly on long journeys. My back was becoming somewhat painful and one can hardly stop on a motorway for a rest! I therefore resolved that any engagements requiring even a relatively long journey would have to be done by train.

Despite these limitations I managed, over the course of the next few years, to fulfil as many speaking obligations as I possibly could, and I was very encouraged by the receptions which I received. Word had, of course, got around in a big way by this time, and the work of AMREF was becoming of far more interest to my audiences than had been the case when I had first started these talks. I was finding that as my energy decreased my audiences increased, and I found this very encouraging indeed.

Naturally, the more engagements I was able to keep over this period the more the funds kept rolling in, and so I continued to make regular visits to our London office. This also enabled me to keep abreast of developments 'on the front line' as well as giving me the opportunity to keep in touch with my AMREF friends in London. By this time Nicola Blundell-Brown had taken up a senior position at the Nairobi headquarters, but I made many new friends at the London office over this period.

By 1989, however, I really did have to make one of the hardest decisions of my life. I was by this time seventy-eight years old; my physical condition had been deteriorating somewhat - particularly my back, and I therefore had to make the very reluctant decision to give up driving my car. I would have hated to be the cause of an accident whilst on my way to a charity fund-raising engagement, and I felt, however sadly, that the time had now come to call a halt to driving.

This was a doubly sad decision. I had, over the years, become very fond of my little 'mini'. Her registration number started with LPH, and I called her 'Little Pocohontas', or Pokey for short. Pokey had been such a regular and loyal companion to me over the course of the last twenty or so years that I am sure that she felt our parting as keenly as I did. However I am happy to say that, unlike her original namesake, the Indian Princess, she did not drown in the river at Gravesend. She is now very happily resettled with a family not more than a mile from my home in North Cheam.

I felt very sad when I visited the London office to tell them of my decision, but I received a wonderfully warm reception there, and was duly thanked for all my hard work over the years. 'Hard work?' I thought to myself - 'to me it's been one long, wonderful holiday!' But I suppose it had been hard work as well.

~O~

That, as I have said, was 1989. How I ever got through the next few years I just do not know. The smell, the taste, the sights, the sounds, the very flavour of Africa was in my veins. I could not reconcile myself to the thought that never again would I see the bush, never again see my friends Dinah and Nelson Kivuti, never again hold babies in the bush for injections, never again feel the wind in my face as I raced in a Piper Cherokee over the deserts and jungles of East Africa. I was going to miss it all so much - and miss it I did!

I still, of course, continued to travel. Over the next few years I received some wonderful invitations to travel abroad - one from a friend in Delaware, USA, whom I had met in Yugoslavia many years previously. Travel breeds friends! I enjoyed this visit tremendously, and here again I had a chance to 'spread the word' for AMREF.

In 1992, whilst on a holiday in the USA, I was taken seriously ill in Albuquerque, New Mexico, having contracted 'Legionnaires Disease' through faulty air-conditioning in a long-distance coach. I was detained for two weeks at a hospital in Albuquerque, followed by an extensive and depressing convalescence back at home. When, the following year, I was again stricken - this time by a strangulated inguinal hernia requiring major surgery - I thought to myself:

'What is the matter with you, Christine? You never used to suffer from all these ailments!'

'The trouble with you,' I replied, 'is that you belong in East Africa. The sooner you get back there the better.'

'I'd better go back, then,' I responded.

So shortly before the Christmas of 1993 I wrote to AMREF in Nairobi. 'I'm coming back,' I said. 'Please book me into the CPK guest house, and please give me something useful to do again.'

I received an unexpectedly prompt reply.

Not only were they longing to see me again, but - it seemed - so were the children at the little school where I had been hailed as the 'rainmaker' all those years ago! They were still very short of basic equipment, including pencils, pens and stationery, and I was asked if I could put a few basic items in my suitcase for these children.

I visited our local stationery shop in North Cheam, Sutton Stationers, and showed them this letter. Their response was magnificent - they virtually denuded their shop of every single colour pencil and pen in their stock. I shall, always be grateful to them.

I also bought up every available suitable item in the little local Oxfam shop where I work as a volunteer.

I borrowed a spare suitcase for the pens and pencils…

I packed my bags…

And off I went.

It was February 1994.

'At last, Christine,' I said to myself, 'you're going back home to where you belong'…

To Africa!

~0~

What a welcome I received when I arrived at the CPK guest house!

Dinah gave me a great big bear-hug, and I was equally warmly received by my other friends - Ruth and Naomi, Charles and the others. As I have already said, the staff were, with few exceptions, the same people as I had met on my first visit, all those years ago in 1974. I was amused to note that President Moi was still relegated to a less prominent position on the office wall, and that my bird embroidery still enjoyed pride of place!

Dinah and Nelson frequently used to organise 'games evenings' at the guest house, where residents take it in turn to give a recital, sing a song, tell a story or whatever else. I remember 'entertaining the troops' on one of these evenings, early on during that stay, with one of my favourite pieces of poetry, 'Temper in October' by V. Edmondson.

'What a pity we don't give prizes,' remarked Dinah. 'You'd have won it hands down!'

I felt very flattered, particularly since not all the guests would have understood it!

I was keen to organise my visit to the school as soon as possible, and to present them with the generous gift of pens and pencils from Sutton Stationers. Very soon, therefore, I was making my way out into the bush in one of the AMREF vans. There was again a most tremendous drought in that part of Kenya, and I hoped that the children would not expect me to make any more rain. I was not too confident of my ability to work a second miracle!

I thought it might be nice to provide something else for the children apart from stationery, and so on my way we stopped at a small shop outside Nairobi and bought two footballs. I thought this might be a novel gift, and it certainly proved to be so.

I received a delightful welcome when I arrived at the school, and I was amazed to find that many of the staff remembered me well, even though it was some eighteen years since my previous visit. I was conducted round the school by the headmaster; it was he who had written to AMREF requesting this return visit, and he showed me a new classroom which AMREF had donated to the school. I was interested to be shown a new water system which the staff had constructed, which was very impressive. I thought this a wonderful example of self-help and enterprise.

We then sat outside, once again under a thorn tree, whilst my gifts were displayed on a table. I explained that many of the pens, pencils and notebooks were gifts from Sutton Stationers in North Cheam, and they were absolutely delighted. Whilst the headmaster distributed these to the various classrooms the children once again treated me to one of their displays of song and dance.

Out they came, once again, class by class. It was an exact repeat of the performance in 1974, and I really did feel that I had been transported back in time. It was a beautiful and touching little occasion, and it was wonderful to feel that these children had gone to all this trouble for my benefit. My mind once again went back to the sequel to the last such occasion, when the heavens had opened and the rain had been produced as if by magic. I don't know whether these children had been told about that incident, but I was relieved when they did not request a repeat performance!

And now it was time to produce my surprise present - the two footballs. The children were absolutely delighted with these, and I am sure that this more than compensated for the lack of magic rain. They waited patiently while they lined up to thank me for my gifts, after which I threw the footballs into their midst. The last I saw of them they were being chased all over the bush, to delighted squeals. Children are children the world over, whether in the suburbs of London or the wilds of the African bush.

When I returned to the guest house I was pleased to discover that my travels were not over for that day. There was a message asking me to contact AMREF headquarters. I phoned Wilson airport and was told that one of their staff had arranged to take me out that afternoon to a small AMREF clinic in the wild country outside the town. This visit proved to be intensely interesting. The clinic was entirely run by AMREF staff, and was quite a long way from the nearest local tribe.

I was shown round the clinic by my AMREF companion, and after this he told me that he wanted to take me out to meet the members of a local tribe, situated about six miles away. 'These people,' he said, 'have something very interesting which they anxious to show you'

Off we went, right out into the wilds, and eventually we arrived at a remote tribal settlement. I was introduced to one of the tribe leaders who escorted me to what looked like a brand new building, still in the course of construction.

This, as it turned out, was a brand new clinic which was being built by the tribe members themselves, entirely on their own initiative. The AMREF clinic being six miles away, the inhabitants were finding this too far for them to travel when they or their families were sick; and so rather than complaining, or appealing to the authorities or to AMREF to provide a more local clinic they had taken the trouble to construct this new little building entirely unaided.

The walls were completed and the roof was still in the course of construction. They had left space for a door and two windows. However they had now run into a problem.

Apparently they had run out of funds, and did not have sufficient money to buy the door and the two windows. They were therefore trying very hard to collect sufficient resources to provide these items and also the wood for the floor.

Apart from these items the clinic was all but completed, and very smart it looked, too. The tribe were clearly very proud indeed of their handiwork, and quite rightly so.

I took my AMREF escort quietly aside, out of earshot, and asked him how much he thought it would cost to provide a door and/or a window for this clinic. I assured him that before I returned home I would give him sufficient money to buy the required door.

He then called the tribe together, and told them that they now had sufficient money to buy their door. He did not, of course, identify the source of the funds, which would have been highly embarrassing, and they were absolutely delighted. In true African tradition they insisted on singing and dancing for me - my second such entertainment that day - and it was wonderful to see them so deliriously happy. I felt about six feet tall.

It was a real pleasure to me to be able to make this small gesture of goodwill. I think that when people go to all this trouble to help themselves - just simple, poor tribespeople - then this really does demonstrate individual enterprise at its very best, and I am certain that it should be encouraged.

My mind went back to that very first meeting with Nicola Blundell-Brown at AMREF's London office, which had led to my first trip to Africa all those years ago and had proved to be my own 'doorway to health'. I thought, somewhat wryly, that there was a certain irony here. Now, twenty two years later, here I was providing this remote Kenyan tribe with their own such doorway - and quite literally so.

'Knock and the door shall be opened.' It was for me, and so it has been for them. The circle was completed, and I was delighted.

When I returned to the guest house that evening I was greeted by my friend Ruth, from the front office.

'And what did you do today?' she asked.

'Amongst other things,' I replied, 'I bought a door.'

Ruth seemed somewhat mystified.

'You bought what?' she asked incredulously.

'A door,' I repeated.

'I didn't see you struggling up the driveway with a door across your shoulders!'

'No,' I quipped. 'After all, I am eighty-two years old, and so I had to leave it behind!'

I then told her the full story, and she was most intrigued. Christine and her door was quite a talking point over the next few days!

There was another interesting talking point that evening. Amongst the guests were two couples from Rwanda, and the conversation turned to the problems of that troubled country.

'Things are going to be much better from now on,' I was told. 'Now we have a good new president, and our troubles will soon be over.'

In the course of the following week a 'plane carrying the new president of Rwanda to Kigali was shot down by terrorists, and the massacres started all over again. I have frequently wondered what became of my Rwandan friends in the end.

Towards the end of that stay in Nairobi I received an unexpected request to attend AMREF headquarters at Wilson Airport. On arrival I was introduced to a group of about eight others and was told that it had been arranged for us all to go on a trip to a clinic and school in Entasopia, near to the Tanzanian border. The others were all also

AMREF representatives, and were from various national branches. The party included representatives from Italy, the United States, Britain, Sweden and Germany. We were therefore quite a multi-national group. There were eleven of us in all, including our two drivers.

We were not told in advance what this was all about, and it therefore appeared to us to be something of a mystery tour. It was an uncomfortably hot day - probably one of the hottest I have ever experienced out in Africa. Our party set off in two vans into the roasting heat of the African bush.

Normally I find no difficulty at all in coping with hot climates - on the contrary they generally suit me very well. However on this occasion the heat was too much even for me, and before we had half completed the journey I really was sweltering. We were told that there was a plentiful supply of cool drinks on the coach, but when these were passed to us the 'cool drinks' were almost too hot to hold!

It was quite a long drive - all down the Great Rift Valley past Lake Magadi - and by the time we reached our destination we were almost melting from the heat. We were welcomed by one of the staff of the clinic who eyed us sympathetically.

'Yes,' he said, without needing to be prompted. 'We do have refreshments for you, 'but first we must do our tree planting.'

'Tree planting? In this heat? What can this all be about?' we thought to ourselves.

We were then conducted around to the side of the building where there was a large open space with eleven recently dug holes. I was relieved that we had been told that we were expected to plant trees, otherwise I might have suspected that these were to be our own graves!

We soon discovered that we were each expected to plant an orange tree to represent our various countries. I was rather pleased that my tree was the second to be planted, which meant that I did not have to hang around for too long in the appalling heat. I really was not feeling at all well by this time!

We were each provided with our tree, a bucket of water and a spade. Each tree had to be planted, earthed in and properly watered. We were then asked to give our names, our personal details and our respective countries so that each tree could be marked with a commemoration plaque. The hope was expressed that in two years time we might be able to return and pluck the first fruits from our orange trees.

I still hope that before very long I shall be able to return and pluck an orange from my very own tree! However at that time all I wanted to do was to get out of the searing heat! We were provided with a meal on the balcony, which I ate very hurriedly and then escaped to the clinic at the first possible opportunity for a lie down. This is the one and only time when I have ever found myself occupying a bed in one of our own clinics, but at least it did give me the opportunity to sample AMREF medical attention at first hand!

After that I was ready to face the long, hot drive back to Nairobi, but on arrival at the CPK guest house I was too exhausted to face dinner. I just wanted my bed, to which I escaped at the earliest possible opportunity.

I was now nearing the end of this, my last trip to East Africa, and very shortly it would be time to pack my bags and say my farewells to my friends for the last time. It was a sad prospect, but there was to be one final treat in store.

On the final Saturday of my visit, just prior to my departure on the following Monday, AMREF gave a gala dinner for friends and supporters, and I felt very honoured to be invited to this function.

I had previously attended one of AMREF's gala dinners, which was held at a very smart hotel in Nairobi. This time, however, the organisers were keen for the occasion to be typically 'AMREF', and so - appropriately, I thought - the dinner was held in a large aircraft hangar at Wilson airport.

When I arrived I was amazed at the transformation. I had only been at this hangar a few days previously. It had then been full of aeroplanes, oil, components and so on - in fact a typical, busy aircraft hangar. How the men got this place cleaned and refurbished ready for a gala dinner I shall never know. But they did.

There was a smart marquee, with tables laid out with the most magnificent buffet dinner. There were over 1000 people present, including staff, guests and their friends. I had invited Dinah and Nelson Kivuti as my guests, and they were truly thrilled to be asked.

After the dinner it was, of course, time for the usual speeches. The Director General, Dr. Michael Gerber, got to his feet and I sat back, eager to hear what he had to say.

After quite a long speech, during which he spoke in detail about AMREF, its history and current projects, he said:

'I have to tell you about one very special guest, who is here tonight and has come all the way from England.'

I was sitting at the same table as John Mramba, who at that time was our Information Officer. John started frantically signalling me to stand up.

'Have you been arranging all this, John?' I asked.

He went into fits of giggles, and - very self-consciously - I duly stood up.

Michael Gerber then launched into a eulogy, recounting my activities on behalf of AMREF over the course of the last twenty two years, and generally thanking me for my efforts. I found it all rather embarrassing, but nevertheless, I thought, it is nice to be appreciated. And then he said something which totally startled me.

'Over the course of this period,' he went on, 'Christine Matthews has been responsible for raising funds to the tune of over forty-five thousand pounds.'

I just couldn't believe it, and I'm still not quite certain that I do! I also thought the eulogy somewhat undeserved. Although it was true that I had done a great deal of work, I had thoroughly enjoyed every minute of it. Be that as it may, on this if no other occasion I appeared to be the celebrity, and I tried to play the part the best I could. After the speeches I took Michael to one side.

'You know, Michael,' I said, 'I'm quite certain that you are exaggerating. I'm quite sure that I never raised anything like that amount. I believe you are crediting me with a great deal of money which I played no part whatsoever in raising.'

'No,' replied Michael. 'Don't accuse me of that. I have carefully checked all your records with the UK office in London, and obtained all your facts and figures from them. They have kept a careful record of all the sums raised by you since you first started working for us in 1972. You can be absolutely certain that the figure I gave was the correct one.

And I think that an organisation that is prepared to go to all that time, trouble and work to sift through all those records so as to ascertain the precise sums raised by one, solitary fund-raiser is certainly well worth working for…

And supporting…

Don't you?

Chapter Eleven

AMREF Today

When Michael Wood first conceived the idea of a Flying Doctor Service for East Africa he could have had little idea of the extent to which his 'brainchild' would grow and expand over the course of the following forty years.

Whilst writing this book I have frequently been prompted to refer to the book which sparked off my own African adventures - Barry Wynne's *Angels on Runway Zero Seven*. It will be remembered that in his book Barry Wynne charts the development of the East African Flying Doctor Service from its early days. Barry Wynne prefaces each chapter with a list of personnel.

In 1960 the organisation consisted of one Medical Director (Michael Wood), one Medical Assistant (American) and one Nursing Sister (Australian). For that year the Service fixed a total budget of £20,000, and owned one single aeroplane. By 1967 the staff had grown to 24 and the budget to £54,000. All but four of the staff were Europeans.

Now, as I write this book, AMREF maintains a staff of over 700, has offices throughout the world and helps to provide health-care and medical services to well over half the African continent. It is interesting - and very encouraging - to note that over 97% of the AMREF staff are themselves Africans.

It is no part of the function of this book to attempt to trace the history and development of this vast organisation; nor do I propose to give more than the briefest outline of its activities. The purpose of embarking on this book was to share my personal reminiscences and to encourage others to 'step into the unknown' and, like me, to find fulfilment in a new life. This was my intention, and I hope that I have gone some way to carrying it out. Here then, perhaps, would be the appropriate time to lay down my pen. 'A cobbler should stick to his last'.

However, if this has been 'my story' it has also been the story of AMREF - the two tales are inseparable. None of my travels and adventures could have been possible had it not been for this wonderful organisation, and I therefore felt it appropriate to close with a brief summary of the functions of AMREF today.

In the early days Michael Wood had, by necessity, to confine himself to providing some sort of emergency medical services to the inhabitants of the Kenyan bush. As we have seen, this soon led to the setting up of a number of field medical stations and clinics, and as the organisation grew the need became apparent for the population to be trained in the provision of 'self-help'. This, as Michael Wood so clearly saw, was the path to a healthier and happier life for the people of this vast continent, and it is a measure of his success that these field hospitals and clinics are now almost entirely manned by the indigenous population. The little tribal clinic near Nairobi which I visited in 1994, and for which I arranged to provide the door, is to me a wonderful example of this 'self-help' in action, and is a real tribute to the initiative and enterprise of these once totally dependent people.

AMREF's efforts are now, therefore, being directed as much to health education and the provision of resources to the individual tribal communities as to the provision of emergency medical treatment and services. The latter does, of course, remain an important part of the foundation's work - 'the flying doctors continue to fly' - but this is now only a part of a wider picture.

To bring health education and disease control to the remote tribes of this vast continent is, of course, a monumental undertaking, and here it must be born in mind that AMREF is a charitable organisation, wholly dependent on voluntary contributions. The task can only be achieved by a careful policy of defining the problems and seeking to provide the solutions stage by stage. To this end AMREF has now embarked upon a five year strategic plan targeting family planning, communicable disease control and prevention, environmental health and emergency service provision.

The area of family planning is of particular importance. The limited resources available cannot hope to keep pace with a population growing at the present rate. Herein lies a difficulty. In past years the men of the tribal communities have refused to accept the very concept of family planning in any form. It was the aim of every tribesman to sire a large family to provide for him in old age, and his sons came to be as much of a status symbol to him as were his cattle. It is difficult to blame him for this. One has only to look back to Victorian times to see identical attitudes prevailing in Britain.

However, it is very encouraging to note that these entrenched attitudes are gradually being broken down, and the dangers of over-population are now beginning to be understood by the communities. To this end AMREF has now embarked on a programme to train 300 family planning trainers from Kenya, Tanzania and Uganda over a period of three years. These trainers will then go on to train literally thousands of staff, who will in turn bring comprehensive family planning to the masses. This is a daunting task, but one which will - more than any other single factor - improve the long term health and happiness of the African.

Incidentally, when I recently visited Kenya in 1994 I decided to try to play my own small part in this initiative. When I visited the Marie Stopes Clinic they taught me how to perform a vasectomy! Readers may be relieved to be assured that I do not have any intention of ever attempting to put this into practice, but it did serve to add to my already vast store of totally useless knowledge!

Disease control and prevention is another enormous undertaking incorporated into the new five year initiative, and will concentrate primarily on the control of malaria, hydatid disease and AIDS. Here again, health education will play a major part in the reduction in the incidence of these largely environmentally spread diseases.

The tremendous task of improving the environment, including the provision of clean water and sanitation, is one of the most daunting challenges facing AMREF today. How this challenge is to be met is, of course, quite outside the scope of this summary. Suffice it to say that a number of initiatives have already been instigated, and that AMREF is working day and night to improve the environment of the population.

And, of course, while all these major hurdles are being steadily surmounted AMREF's dedicated team of flying doctors continue their daily flights 'into the bush,' bringing their medical and surgical skills to the remote tribes of Africa.

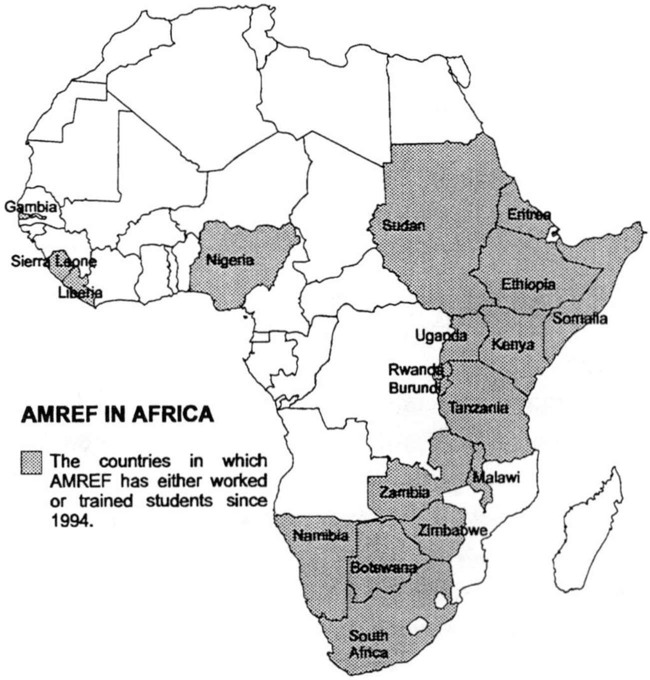

When Michael Wood embarked on this project he was, at best, able to bring medical help to a small area of Kenya. As will be seen from the map on the previous page, AMREF now covers well over half of the African continent, and now extends its activities right down to South Africa.

Herein lies another challenge for AMREF. The recent, hard-won and welcome independence of South Africa has brought with it its own medical problems. Whereas previously the available resources of that unhappy country were concentrated largely on the small minority of Europeans, now the same resources are expected to cover the needs of the entire population. Here again AMREF has stepped in, and is continuing to provide what assistance it can.

This, then, is the situation facing AMREF today. Such a gargantuan undertaking does, of course, require a finely integrated network of field hospitals, clinics, medical centres and administrative headquarters spread across the continent. In addition to its main headquarters at Nairobi AMREF has main regional offices in Dar-es-Salaam, Tanzania, Kampala, Uganda and Pretoria, South Africa. Within Kenya itself, in addition to the many clinics and field hospitals AMREF maintains three main regional medical centres, respectively at Kibwezi in the south-east, Lopiding in the north and Entasopia, near lake Magadi. It is this latter centre, at Entasopia, which I visited in 1994, and where I planted my orange tree prior to collapsing from the heat on an AMREF bed!

I still intend, God willing, to keep my promise of plucking an orange from my very own tree! And when that happens I still hope, once again, to fly in an AMREF 'plane and see again at first hand the work which continues to be done by this magnificent organisation.

This time I shall, no doubt, take a more passive role - I fear that my time for holding babies for injections and spraying bush surgeries with insecticide may now be over - but I will continue to try to do what I can. Whatever happens I refuse to throw in my hand until I have once again seen all my wonderful friends - Anne Spoerry (still flying her little Cherokee on regular journeys into the bush), Nicky Blundell-Brown (now International Co-ordinator for AMREF in Nairobi) and, of course, my very dear friends Dinah and Nelson Kivuti. Life will not be complete without seeing them all once again.

So that is my story. The story of one library book which gave me a new life. What a life it has been, and what a privilege it has been for me to work for such an organisation, and alongside such wonderful and inspired people.

I remember asking Michael Wood, as we were flying down to Singida that day back in 1976, how he would have felt if he had known, in advance, how his small Flying Doctor Service would expand so explosively in the years to come.

'I think,' he replied, 'that I would have turned tail and fled!'

In his position, who could have blamed him?

But I'm very glad he didn't!

Epilogue

'Karibu Tena'

'Karibu Tena,' said Anne Spoerry when writing her charming foreword to this book. 'Come again soon.' And so I did.

However, there was a time, back in 1994, when I was quite convinced that never again would I travel to Africa or anywhere else. For in September of that year I suffered a major stroke, and for the several weeks while I was in hospital there was considerable doubt as to whether I would even be allowed to return home.

These were dark days indeed.

It all started off with what I thought was nothing worse than a bad attack of migraine. The Doctor was called, and he advised me to rest and to call him again if there was no improvement. When, later that day, the condition worsened and I started to feel disorientated a neighbour called the Doctor out again, and the next thing I remember was waking up in hospital.

'Has anybody told you that you've had a stroke?' asked one of the nurses some days later.

A stroke! To me it seemed as if my whole world had come to an end. Having nursed my husband through the aftermath of a stroke I knew only too well what this could lead to. The strange thing was that I seemed to be able to speak quite rationally, whereas my husband had lost his power of speech almost entirely.

As it turned out I was extremely lucky. The haemorrhage which had caused my stroke had not, apparently, affected the speech centre, and my speech was therefore relatively unaffected. Had I been unable to speak I really do not think I could have faced life again.

However, I discovered that I had almost completely lost control of my limbs, and after the initial recuperation period I had to undergo intense physiotherapy to learn to walk again. I cannot speak too highly of the physiotherapists at the hospital. With infinite patience they coaxed me, cajoled me and - sometimes - bullied me into walking - first a few steps at a time and then progressing to longer walks and, ultimately, stairs. It was a long, slow process but in the end it paid undreamed of dividends, to the extent that I am now very nearly back to full mobility. I will never forget the wonderful work of that team of physiotherapists.

After some eight weeks I was allowed to return home, and continued to improve in strength and mobility day by day. However, very much to my disappointment I discovered that my sight had deteriorated to such an extent that I was unable to continue with my fine embroidery - for so long such a favourite hobby of mine. I tried very hard to overcome this problem, but it would seem that one of the long term effects of my stroke had been severe damage to one of my optic nerves, and very reluctantly I had to accept that embroidery would have to be a thing of the past. 'No more bird embroideries to replace President Moi on Dinah's office wall,' I thought to myself wryly!

But I had to do something! I just could not face the prospect of sitting all day reading books and staring at my living room wall. When one has been so active for so long enforced immobility is even harder to face.

It was my son who came up with a possible solution, when he remarked to me one day, shortly after my return home, 'Why don't you set about writing that book?'

For many years various people had been trying to persuade me to write a book about my experiences and travels with AMREF, and I certainly thought that these would make an interesting and worthwhile narrative if I could ever find the time to get round to it. The trouble was that there had hardly ever been a spare moment to write a letter - let alone a book! For some twenty years life had been one long hectic round of travels to Africa and lecture tours. Now God had intervened in the most unexpected way, and perhaps this was His way of telling me to slow down! It is certainly very unlikely that if I had not been taken ill this book would ever have been written.

In any event, I thought to myself, this would be one way of occupying my time, even if nothing ever came of it. So I happily set myself to the task of sifting through my old memories and records, from those early days in 1971 through to that last, happy reunion with my AMREF friends in February 1994, and slowly, piece by piece, this book started to take shape. This little volume is the result, and I hope readers will have enjoyed reading it as much as I have enjoyed my first, tentative steps as an author!

After I had completed the drafts of the first few chapters I sent these to Anne Spoerry in Nairobi for her advice and opinion, and very kindly she offered to write the Foreword. '*Karibu Tena*,' as she said. 'Come back again.' This was too good an opportunity to miss, and as soon as I was fit enough to travel I was once again winging my way back to Nairobi. This time I was accompanied by my son - I thought that I should have someone to hand just in case , and in any event he was keen to see the work of AMREF at first hand, having heard so much from me about it all over the years.

This time, instead of a camera my flight bag contained the completed proofs of my new book. I could not wait to see how it would be received by my friends in Nairobi.

Karibu Tena...

I was coming back!

It was wonderful to be back at my 'second home' - the CPK Guest House where, true to form, we arrived in the middle of a severe drought. There was a very severe shortage of water in the guest house and the staff were, as usual, struggling heroically against tremendous odds. It was wonderful to see many of my old friends again - Naomi the receptionist, Freda the housekeeper, Nancy and many others whom I remembered from my previous trips. Dinah and Nelson were away in America when we first arrived, attending a family wedding, and we were greeted instead by Grace Wombui, a charming lady who has now taken over as manager so as to enable Dinah and Nelson to concentrate on a new initiative - an impressive youth training project for the Church of the Province of Kenya.

On our first evening at the Guest House we were visited by Nicola Blundell-Brown, who had drawn up what looked like a most exhausting schedule of trips out to various AMREF enterprises. The following day we met her for lunch at the Aero Club at Wilson Airport to discuss this schedule, and the result was a most enjoyable and rewarding opportunity to see once again many aspects of the work of this magnificent organisation.

Two particularly interesting visits were to the Kimuka School and the Childrens' Home at Kajiado.

It was at the primary school at Kimuka that I had been hailed as a rainmaker all those years ago, and it was fascinating to see once again the work being carried out there. Maurice, the headmaster, took us on a conducted tour of the school, and once again the children, class by class, entertained us in song. Some of the children even remembered me from my previous visit in 1994 - although those who had watched entranced as I 'made the rain' have now long since grown up. It seemed strange to reflect that many of them may now be the parents of the current pupils!

Daniel Sapoya's workshop at Kajiado has now been extensively equipped with new machinery and tools, and he proudly demonstrated to us how he is now able to make jointed callipers. Previously he had only been able to manufacture rigid callipers, which enabled the children to walk but not to sit with any degree of comfort. These disabled children gave us a wonderful welcome, and later emulated the schoolchildren at Kimuka by singing to us in their classrooms. 'Twinkle, twinkle little star' sounds rather strange when delivered in a mixture of Swahili and broken English! Muteti, our driver for that day, was able to give me a most interesting appraisal of the work currently being undertaken by AMREF's nomadic unit, and I was once again highly impressed to realise what enormous progress has been made since those early years when Michael Wood first had his 'vision'.

Anne Spoerry was kind enough to entertain us for lunch at her lovely home in Muthaiga, a residential district of Nairobi. Now in her late seventies, Anne has lost none of her energy and dedication, and she still remains in charge of the mobile unit, making daily forays in to the bushlands. We were very privileged when 'Mama Daktari,' as she is known to many of the locals, agreed to be interviewed on video camera. Anne very rarely gives interviews, and my son listened with fascination as she told us the story of her many years with AMREF.

Shortly before leaving England I had invested in a rather expensive hearing aid, and this very nearly came to a very strange end! We were taken out one day for a drive in the Nairobi Game Park. The usual transport, a Forest Range Rover, was not available that day, and instead we were taken out in a very rickety and unstable 'taxi'. On my return to the guest house I discovered that my hearing aid was missing. The following day my son made a frantic visit to the office of the tour company. The driver was located, who remembered finding in the back of his vehicle, the previous day, what he had taken to be a small Masai bead. I suspect that had we left it much longer before recovering it my precious hearing aid would by now be adorning the neck of a Masai Tribesman!

But instead, it was I who returned home the proud possessor of a beautiful necklace of African beads. Lady Wood, Michael's widow, presented me with this when we visited her at her lovely home 'Kazuri,' where she maintains a little workshop with a small kiln, where local people are instructed in the art of making these beautiful

'Kazuri beads'. I was presented with a most attractive red and pink necklace of Kazuri beads, which I often wear as a reminder of that final, lovely trip to my good friends in Nairobi.

Did I say 'final'?

I wonder?

They only have to say '*Karibu Tena*'...

And perhaps I will!

INDEX

Glossary

AMREF	The African Medical and Research Foundation.
Baobab	The large, 'upside down' tree, native to Africa.
Canthaxanthin	A chemical substance found in the algae of the Kenyan soda lakes.
Hydatid disease	A parasitic cystic disease particularly prevalent among the Turkana tribe of Northern Kenya.
Inner Wheel	The ladies' branch of the Rotary Organisation.
Karibu tena	Swahili: 'Come again'.
Lakes Magadi and Natron	The great soda lakes of Central and Southern Africa.
Manyatta	A small adobe-style hut lived in by the Masai.
Masai (tribe)	A nomadic tribe of the highlands of Kenya and Tanzania.
Matoke	A dish consisting of mashed banana or plantain.
Musth	A stage in the reproductive cycle of the male elephant.
Pocho	Maize porridge eaten widely in East Africa.
Trefoil Guild	The National Guild of the Girl Guides Movement.
Turkana (tribe)	A tribe centred in the region of the Kenya/Ethiopia borders.
Uhuru	Swahili: 'Freedom'.

Note

Any donations to the African Medical and Research Foundation may be sent to:-

- AMREF, 11, Old Queen Street, London SW1H 9JA

- AMREF, PO Box No. 30125, Wilson Airport, Nairobi, Kenya.

- AMREF, 19 West 44th Street, #1708, New York, USA

Vitalstoffreiche Rezepte für mehr Energie, Anti-Aging und ein gutes Immunsystem

DIANA PYTER

Saftladen

freya

Inhalt

Rezepte ab Seite 57 →

Rezepte

VIDEO
Seite 73

VIDEO
Seite 80

VIDEO
Seite 96

VIDEO
Seite 115

VIDEO
Seite 140

VIDEO
Seite 160

Vorwort

Möchten Sie den einfachsten Tipp wissen, wie man schnell seinen Energielevel, sein Immunsystem, seine Ausstrahlung und Gesundheit verbessern kann? Der Zaubertrunk ist ein Glas frisch gepresster Saft – die einfachste Möglichkeit, den Körper rasant mit einer großen Menge an Vitalstoffen zu fluten und ihn damit nachhaltig zu energetisieren und zu revitalisieren.

Ich selbst bin vor vielen Jahren in Kalifornien *auf den Saft* gekommen. Galt früher der Coffee to go als Must-have beim Shoppingbummel, auf dem Weg zum Büro oder nach dem Workout, so ist es heute längst der frisch gepresste Saft – vorzugsweise in Giftgrün. In den letzten Jahren ist der Shot dazugekommen, der kleine und konzentrierte Bruder des frisch gepressten Saftes. Ein großer Schluck davon beinhaltet oft mehr Vitalstoffe, als so mancher Obst- und Gemüsemuffel in einer ganzen Woche zu sich nimmt. Ich war von der Vielfalt der Säfte und Shots – eine tolle und leichte Alternative zu den Smoothies – sofort begeistert, denn bereits beim ersten Schluck merkte ich, wie mein Körper, meine Zellen frohlockten und dieses flüssige Elixier wie ein Schwamm aufsogen. Meine Familie und ich konnten nicht genug von den köstlichen Obst- und Gemüsemischungen bekommen und wir fühlten uns mit jedem Tag frischer und energiereicher, was natürlich auch zu einem Teil an der Sonne Kaliforniens liegt. Die frisch gepressten Säfte aus den Juice-Bars, die es mittlerweile an allen Ecken wie Coffeeshops gibt, zogen uns in ihren Bann und wir wollten diesen energetisierenden Lifestyle auch im heimischen Deutschland weiterleben. Schließlich gilt es, Tag für Tag große Herausforderungen mit möglichst viel Elan und Energie zu meistern: Kinder und Jugendliche den Stress in Schule und Studium, Frauen die Doppelbelastung von Beruf und Haushalt, Männer die vielen Herausforderungen im Berufsalltag und nebenbei sollte man sich auch bestmöglich um den eigenen Körper kümmern, sich gut ernähren und fit bleiben.

Schnell war eine geeignete Saftpresse gefunden, es wurden Rezepte getestet, optimiert und ständig haben wir mit neuen Mischungen und Varianten experimentiert. Entstanden ist ein ganzes Sammelsurium an leckeren Säften, Smoothies, Shots, Suppen, Breien und Eiscremes, die hier im Buch vorgestellt werden. Denn: Es gibt zwar mittlerweile auch hierzulande in den Supermärkten ein großes Angebot an Säften und Smoothies, aber an den herrlichen Geschmack und die Nährstoff-Fülle von frisch gepressten Obst- und Gemüsemixturen kommt kein noch so gutes Fertigprodukt heran. Und das Beste: Diese Elixiere mit frischem Obst, Gemüse, Nüssen, Samen und Kräutern sind in Minutenschnelle verdaut und die besten und natürlichsten Nahrungsergänzungsmittel der Welt.

Im ausführlichen Info-Teil erfährt man außerdem jede Menge darüber, wie man täglich die Pflanzenpower nutzen, auf einfache Art und Weise mehr vitalstoffreiche Lebensmittel in seine Ernährung integrieren und sich damit gesünder, vitaler, schöner und voller Energie fühlen kann. Darüber hinaus gibt es viele Tipps zum Saftfasten, saisonalem Essen, natürlichem Anti-Aging und man erfährt, welche Entsafter sich am besten für frisch gepresste Säfte, Smoothies, Shots und Suppen eignen. Dieses Buch wird Klein wie Groß und Jung wie Alt jede Menge Spaß dabei machen, täglich ausreichend Obst und Gemüse in all seiner bunten Vielfalt zu genießen. Hier geht es nicht um Kalorienzählen, sondern darum, den Gaumen mit gesunden Lebensmitteln zu verwöhnen und den Körper zu revitalisieren.

Ich wünsche viel Spaß beim Entdecken der frisch gepressten Säfte, leckeren Smoothies, köstlichen Suppen, intensiven Shots und erfrischenden Eiscremes voller Vitalstoffe.

Diana Pyter

» **VIDEO**
Kalifornien-Flair

Du bist, was du isst

Wie ernährst du deinen Körper, deine 100 Billionen Zellen? Mit frischen, vitalstoffreichen Lebensmitteln – also viel Obst und Gemüse – oder mit eingepackten, eingeschweißten und stark verarbeiteten Gerichten voller Chemikalien? Du bist, was du isst, sagt ein gängiges Sprichwort. Aus dem Essen, mit dem man seinen Körper ernährt, bastelt er neue Zellen. Sekunde um Sekunde, Tag für Tag, Jahr für Jahr, damit die Maschine Mensch optimal laufen kann.

Idealerweise sollten täglich fünf bis sieben Portionen Obst und Gemüse konsumiert werden, um dem Körper alle notwendigen Vitalstoffe wie Vitamine, Mineralstoffe, Enzyme, Amino- und Fettsäuren sowie sekundäre Pflanzenstoffe zur Verfügung zu stellen. Diese benötigt er für den reibungslosen Ablauf aller Körperfunktionen und um fit und gesund zu bleiben. Hand aufs Herz: Wer konsumiert wirklich diese große Menge an Obst und Gemüse, die Gesundheitsorganisationen zur Erhaltung der Gesundheit vorschlagen? Leider nur die wenigsten. Fünf bis sieben Por-

tionen Obst und Gemüse müssen jedoch keine unüberwindbare Hürde sein, denn mit frisch gepressten Säften, Smoothies, Powershots und Suppen lässt sich das durchaus realisieren. So enthalten zwei Gläser frisch gepresster Saft bereits die erstrebenswerte Menge! Wer fit, vital und gesund bleiben möchte, sollte also Augenmerk darauf legen, lieber die zugeführten Vitalstoffe als die Kalorien zu zählen.

Natürlich ist es nicht ganz einfach, von alten Gewohnheiten Abschied zu nehmen, Gedankenmuster zu durchbrechen und vor allem den inneren Schweinehund zu überwinden. Langfristig wird sich das Umdenken hin zu einer gesünderen Lebensweise aber auf alle Fälle auszahlen. Schließlich nutzen wir den ganzen Tag die unglaublichen Fähigkeiten des Körpers. Er läuft mit uns meilenweit, trägt die schwersten Taschen, entdeckt mit uns traumhafte und farbintensive Landschaften, hört mit uns die schönste Musik, erlebt mit uns die tollsten Glücksgefühle, riecht die schönsten Düfte und denkt mit uns den ganzen Tag. Erst wenn es einmal nicht mehr so gut läuft, kommt man ins Grübeln, dass man mehr Rücksicht auf den Körper nehmen und ihm mehr Gutes tun könnte.

Was passiert, wenn man seinem Körper wirklich die Lebensmittel gibt, die er haben möchte, um daraus starke und voll funktionstüchtige Zellen zu basteln? Die Haare werden kräftiger und glänzender, die Sehschärfe kann sich verbessern, die Haut frischer und praller wirken, das Herz ruhiger und gleichmäßiger schlagen, Konzentration und Reaktionsfähigkeit können sich steigern. Man fühlt sich wieder voller Energie und viel leistungsfähiger.

Man muss aber nicht sofort über Nacht zum Vegetarier, Veganer oder Rohköstler mutieren. Vielmehr geht es in diesem Ratgeber darum, wie man täglich auf einfache Art und Weise mehr vitalstoffreiche Lebensmittel zu sich nehmen und den Körper damit richtig ernähren kann.

Warum ist Rohkost so gesund?

Pflanzenpower effektiv nutzen

Frische und unveränderte Lebensmittel wie Obst, Gemüse, Samen, Nüsse, Sprossen und Kräuter haben aus ernährungsphysiologischer Sicht die höchste Wertigkeit für unseren Körper. Die rohköstliche Nahrung weist einen großen Anteil an Vitaminen, Mineralstoffen, Spurenelementen, Aminosäuren, sekundären Pflanzenstoffen und Enzymen auf. Frisches Obst und Gemüse aus dem Eigenanbau oder als Bioware sind zudem weniger mit Schadstoffen belastet und damit frei von chemischen Zusatzstoffen, wie sie verarbeitete Lebensmittel oft beinhalten.

Wie kraftvoll eine pflanzenbasierte Ernährung ist, sieht man an den größten und stärksten Tieren der Erde. Elefanten, Gorillas, Büffel, Pferde oder Nashörner ernähren sich ausschließlich von pflanzenbasierter Kost, die aus rohen Blättern, Gras und Früchten besteht. Auch der Mensch kann von einer Ernährung, die viel Rohkost beinhaltet, maßgeblich profitieren.

Die einzige Hürde bei der Pflanzennahrung besteht darin, dass man an die in den harten Zellwänden eingeschlossenen Nährstoffe gelangt. Dies erreicht man entweder durch intensives Kauen oder durch Hilfsmittel wie Entsafter oder Mixer. Entsafter erledigen für den Körper quasi die Vorarbeit, denn sie extrahieren die Nährstoffe und das Wasser – genau wie das der Darm auch macht. Der große Vorteil von Entsaftern gegenüber Mixern besteht jedoch darin, dass sie zum einen die schwer verdaulichen Faserstoffe abtrennen und zum anderen viel schonender, das heißt mit weniger Umdrehungen arbeiten. So bleiben die Nährstoffe optimal erhalten, denn es kommt aufgrund der sanften Verarbeitung zu keiner Hitze-Entwicklung und weniger Oxidation beim Verarbeitungsprozess.

Vor allem die natürlichen Enzyme, welche in frischem Obst und Gemüse enthalten sind, ermöglichen es dem Körper, Lebensmittel einfa-

cher und schneller zu verdauen. Enzyme sind für sämtliche Körperfunktionen notwendig. Bei stark gekochten oder verarbeiteten Lebensmitteln sind diese Enzyme größtenteils zerstört, denn ab ca. 45 Grad verlieren sie ihre Wirkkraft. Unser Verdauungssystem muss folglich erst Verdauungsenzyme bilden, um die Nahrung aufzuspalten und ihr alle wichtigen Nährstoffe zu entnehmen. Das kostet Energie, die der Körper für viele andere wichtige Stoffwechsel-Prozesse benötigt. Und genau diese Kraft für eine gute Verdauungsarbeit hat er eben, wenn wir die natureigenen Enzyme von Obst und Gemüse nicht durch Braten, Kochen, Raffinieren oder Frittieren zerstören, sondern sie möglichst in Form von Rohkost konsumieren und nur schonend verarbeiten, wie dies unter anderem beim Entsaften, Dämpfen oder Dünsten der Fall ist. Eine Ernährung mit einem großen Anteil von Rohkost stellt zudem sicher, dass der Körper eine Vielzahl an Enzymen erhält, die der Stoffwechsel zum Aufbau, zur Reinigung und Gesunderhaltung des Körpers benötigt.

Frisch zubereitete und schonend hergestellte Säfte, Smoothies und Suppen haben daher große Vorteile für die Gesunderhaltung des Körpers. Sie sind nicht nur geballte Nährstoff-Energie, sondern damit lassen sich auch die Empfehlungen von Gesundheitsorganisationen, täglich fünf bis sieben Portionen Obst und Gemüse (eine Portion entspricht einer Handvoll) zu essen, relativ einfach umsetzen. Um dieselbe Menge an Vitaminen, Enzymen, Mineral- und Pflanzennährstoffen wie z. B. in einem Glas frisch gepressten Saft zu sich zu nehmen, müsste man ungefähr die dreifache Menge an Obst und Gemüse im Ganzen essen. Das ist sehr viel und in der Realität schaffen das nicht viele Menschen. Säfte, Smoothies, Suppen oder Power-Shots sind daher eine einfache Möglichkeit, ausreichend Rohkost zu konsumieren und so den Körper mit einer Vielzahl an Vitalstoffen zu versorgen.

Durch die Verarbeitung von Obst und Gemüse wie z. B. langes Braten, Kochen, Raffinieren oder Frittieren werden nicht nur die Enzyme zerstört, sondern teilweise auch wertvolle Vitamine, Mineral- und Pflanzenstoffe.

› Durch Kochen verringert sich der Vitamin-C-Gehalt von Lebensmitteln, günstiger sind Dämpfen und Dünsten.

› Lange Warmhalte- und Lagerzeiten zerstören ebenfalls viele Vitalstoffe.

› Mineralstoffe und wasserlösliche Vitamine wie B-Vitamine waschen sich in die Kochflüssigkeit aus. Besser: Suppen und Eintöpfe, da hierbei die Flüssigkeit mitgegessen wird.

› Der Gehalt an Antioxidantien, die für den Zellschutz wichtig sind, sinkt durch Erhitzen erheblich.

› Nach 10 Min. im Kochwasser haben verschiedene Gemüsesorten wie z. B. Spinat einen Großteil aller sekundären Pflanzenstoffe an das Kochwasser abgegeben.

› Ernährung kann entweder vor Krankheiten schützen oder diese verursachen. Rohkost fördert die Gesundheit, verarbeitete Lebensmittel wie Fast Food können bei übermäßigem Konsum zu Krankheiten führen.

Bunt ist gesund

Die Farben des Regenbogens essen

Idealerweise sollte man täglich Obst und Gemüse in den unterschiedlichsten Farben zu sich nehmen – am besten jeweils eine Portion in Gelb, Rot, Lila, Weiß und Grün. Für frisch gepresste Obst- und Gemüsesäfte, Smoothies, Suppen und Power-Shots kann man die bunten Farben wunderbar kombinieren und dem Körper eine Vielfalt an Vitaminen, Mineralien, Enzymen, Aminosäuren und Pflanzenstoffen wie zum Beispiel zellschützenden Antioxidantien liefern. Jede einzelne Farbe hält unter-

schiedliche Vitalstoffe bereit und daher ist es so wichtig, das ganze Spektrum des Regenbogens zu nutzen. Man darf und sollte es also bunt treiben, wenn es um Obst und Gemüse geht.

TIPP

Ideal sind saisonale und regionale Lebensmittel, da sie reif geerntet, nur kurz gelagert und frisch angeboten werden. Somit liefern sie ein Maximum an Vitalstoffen.

ROT

Rotes Obst und Gemüse sind reich an Lycopin. Dieser Pflanzenfarbstoff zählt zu den Antioxidantien und gilt als Radikalfänger, d. h. zellschädigende Moleküle werden im Körper unschädlich gemacht. Außerdem wirken rotes Obst und Gemüse anregend und belebend. Sie unterstützen die Herzgesundheit, das gesamte Herz-Kreislaufsystem und den Zellschutz. Auch der Gefäßverstopfung sowie der Haut- und Zellalterung kann damit vorgebeugt werden.

Obst: *Granatäpfel, Erdbeeren, Himbeeren, Kirschen, Wassermelonen, Preiselbeeren, Johannisbeeren, Cranberries*
Gemüse: *Tomaten, Rote Bete, roter Paprika, Radieschen, Hagebutten*
Gewürze: *Chili, Pfeffer*

GELB – ORANGE

Gelbes oder oranges Obst und Gemüse sind reich an Vitamin C, Beta-Carotin, Alpha-Carotin und Antioxidantien.

Für die Gelb- oder Orangefärbung sind Carotinoide verantwortlich, die eine Pflanze auch vor UV-Strahlen schützen. Carotinoide sind Antioxidantien, die freie Radikale unschädlich machen und so vielen Erkrankungen und der Hautalterung vorbeugen. Sie stärken außerdem das Immunsystem und helfen bei Entzündungen. Gelbe oder orange Früchte bzw. Gemüse sollten idealerweise mit guten Fetten (wie z. B. Avocado, Kokos- oder Olivenöl) gegessen werden, da Carotinoide fettlöslich sind und dies die Resorption verbessert. Carotinoide werden vom Körper in Vitamin A umgewandelt, was wiederum unsere Sehkraft stärkt.

Obst: *Bananen, gelbe Äpfel, Mangos, Ananas, Zitronen, Orangen, Grapefruits, Mirabellen, gelbe Pflaumen, gelbe Birnen, Papayas, Sanddorn*
Gemüse: *Kürbis, Möhren, Mais, Pastinaken, Süßkartoffeln, gelbe Zucchini, gelbe Paprika*
Gewürze/Kräuter: *Kurkuma, Ingwer, Vanille*

GRÜN

Grüne Lebensmittel sind reich an Vitamin C, Antioxidantien, Flavonoiden, Kalium, Selen, Vitamin K und enthalten viel Chlorophyll – das Blut der Pflanzen. Chlorophyll ist ähnlich wie Hämoglobin aufgebaut und kann daher bewirken, dass im Körper mehr Sauerstoff transportiert wird. Grüne Lebensmittel neutralisieren, wirken alkalisch und reinigend.

Obst: *Äpfel, Birnen, Stachelbeeren, Limonen, Limetten, Kiwis, Feigen, grüne Trauben*
Gemüse: *Avocados, Artischocken, Bohnen, Brokkoli, Erbsen, Gurken, Salat, Oliven, Paprika, Spinat, Zucchini, Porree, Mangold, Kohlrabi, Kohl*
Gewürze/Kräuter: *alle grünen Kräutersorten wie Petersilie, Basilikum, Dill, Kerbel, Schnittlauch, Minze, Kresse, Rosmarin, Estragon, Wildkräuter*

LILA

Für die Blaufärbung sorgen Anthocyane – ein Flavonoid (sekundärer Pflanzenstoff) und eine wahre Anti-Aging-Wunderwaffe. Flavonoide sind gut für Gehirn, Herz und Haut. Sie schützen vor UV-Strahlen, binden freie Radikale, sind entzündungshemmend und gefäßschützend.

Obst: *Brombeeren, rote Stachelbeeren, schwarze Johannisbeeren, Feigen, Heidelbeeren, Holunderbeeren, Pflaumen, blaue Weintrauben*
Gemüse: *Auberginen, rote Zwiebeln, Rotkohl, Radicchio, Lollo rosso, Kohlrabi*
Gewürze/Kräuter: *Salbei, Thymian, Borretsch*

WEISS

Weißes Obst und Gemüse enthalten starke Antioxidantien, bekämpfen Infektionen, reinigen und stärken die Abwehr. Außerdem wirken sie entzündungshemmend, gefäßschützend und fördern die Durchblutung.
Obst: *Litschi*
Gemüse: *Spargel, Knoblauch, Zwiebeln, Chicorée, Rettich, Blumenkohl, Fenchel, Champignons, Lauch, Sellerie, Meerrettich*

» **VIDEO**
Wie bereitet man grüne Säfte zu?

Formen von Obst und Gemüse:

und ihr Bezug zu Körperorganen

Schon vor über 2 000 Jahren hat Hippokrates, der Urvater der Medizin, darauf aufmerksam gemacht, dass Nahrung eine starke therapeutische Wirkung haben kann und dass Früchten, Gemüse, Kräutern und Gewürzen eine unglaubliche Heilkraft innewohnt. „Unsere Nahrungsmittel sollten Heilmittel, unsere Heilmittel Nahrungsmittel sein", lautete seine Aussage.

Wenn man Obst und Gemüse genau betrachtet, erinnern viele Sorten aufgrund ihrer Formen und Farben an die Körperorgane des Menschen, die sie wirkungsvoll unterstützen können. Sie liefern jede Menge Powerstoffe aus der Natur bzw. Inhaltsstoffe, die genau für dieses Körperorgan förderlich sind.

Tomate: ist rot und hat vier Kammern wie unser Herz – Herznahrung (u. a.aufgrund von hohem Lycopin-Anteil)

Avocados/Auberginen/Birnen: sehen aus wie die Gebärmutter – Avocados unterstützen den Hormonhaushalt der Frau und schützen die Unterleibsorgane (Avocado benötigt von der Blüte bis zur Reife ca. 9 Monate)

Trauben: haben die Form von Blutzellen und sehen auch wie Lungenbläschen aus – sind gut für das Blut, die Lunge und bei Asthma

Feigen: ähneln den Hoden – hängen paarweise am Baum und beinhalten tausende Samen; können Mobilität der Spermien steigern und bei Unfruchtbarkeit helfen

Oliven und Granatapfel: haben Formen wie die Eierstöcke bzw. die Follikel in den Eierstöcken – unterstützen die Fortpflanzungsorgane

Walnuss: erinnert an das Gehirn – Gehirn- und Nervennahrung (viel Omega-3-Fettsäuren, Folsäure, Vitamin E)

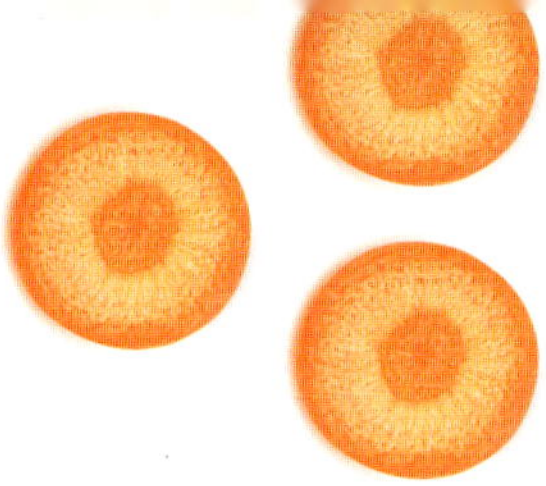

Sellerie/Rhabarber, Blätterkohl: innen weiß, ähneln optisch einem Knochen – Knochennahrung

Möhren: sehen aufgeschnitten wie ein Auge mit Pupille aus – Augennahrung (durch hohen Anteil von Beta-Karotin)

Ingwer: sieht aus wie der menschliche Magen – natürliches Heilmittel bei Magenproblemen (Gingerole hemmen Helicobacter, steigern die Magensaftsekretion und Darmperistaltik)

Süßkartoffel: ähnlich der Form der Bauchspeicheldrüse – unterstützt die Bauchspeicheldrüse durch B-Vitamine und Mineralstoffe

Pilze: sehen aufgeschnitten wie ein Ohr aus – gut für die Gesundheit der Ohren (Vitamin D)

Bohnen: haben die Form von Nieren – unterstützen die Nierenfunktion

Orangen und Zitrusfrüchte: ähneln den Milchdrüsen der Brust – fördern die Gesundheit der Brüste und den Lymphfluss (Vitamine C, B, Mineralstoffe und Spurenelemente)

Spargel: potenzfördernd durch zahlreiche Mineralstoffe und Spurenelemente

Geballte Nährstoff-Konzentrationen

in einer Mahlzeit

Frisch gepresste Säfte, Smoothies, Suppen und Shots beinhalten eine hohe Konzentration an verschiedenen wichtigen Nährstoffen, wie z. B. Vitaminen, Mineralstoffen, Proteinen, Fetten, Kohlenhydraten sowie sekundären Pflanzenstoffen, aber auch Wasser und Sauerstoff. Obst- und Gemüsemischungen in Rohkost-Qualität sind daher äußerst wertvolle Nahrungsmittel und essentielle Nährstoff-Lieferanten.

Nachfolgend ein Überblick über die wichtigsten Nährstoffe für den menschlichen Körper.

Kohlenhydrate

sind ein Produkt der Photosynthese der Pflanzen und bilden den größten Teil der Biomasse auf der Erde. Kohlenhydrate werden vom Körper zu Glukose abgebaut und liefern ihm Energie. Sie gehören zu den zentralen Energieträgern und sind ein wesentlicher Bestandteil der menschlichen Nahrung. Hohe Kohlenhydrat-Anteile finden sich in Getreideprodukten, Kartoffeln sowie Hülsenfrüchten. Es gibt Monosaccharide (Einfachzucker wie Trauben- und Fruchtzucker), Disaccharide (Zweifachzucker wie Kristallzucker, Milchzucker) und Oligosaccharide (Raffinose) sowie Polysaccharide (Vielfachzucker wie Stärke, Cellulose).

Gute Kohlenhydrat-Lieferanten:

Früchte, Körner, Bohnen, Wurzelgemüse

Proteine

bestehen aus Aminosäuren. Einige kann der Körper selbst herstellen, andere müssen mit der Nahrung zugeführt werden. Proteine haben eine strukturelle und funktionale Rolle. Sie sind wichtig für den Aufbau neuer Zellen und für Reparaturvorgänge im Körper. Alle Zellen beinhalten Proteine, sie transportieren aber auch Stoffwechselprodukte oder beschleunigen chemische Reaktionen. Alle Proteine stammen von Pflanzen, tierische Proteine sind lediglich recycelte Pflanzenproteine. Proteine aus Pflanzen haben eine gute Bioverfügbarkeit.

Gute Protein-Lieferanten: *Körner und Samen wie Quinoa, grünes Blattgemüse, Samen, Nüsse, Bohnen, Linsen, Spirulina, Chlorella, Eier, Fisch, Joghurt, Quark*

Fette

bestehen aus Fettsäuren (gesättigt & ungesättigt), die u. a. als Energielieferanten dienen und Lösungsmittel für fettlösliche Vitamine, Schutzpolster und ein Bestandteil der Zellmembran sind.

Gute Fettsäure-Lieferanten: *Samen, Nüsse, Mandeln, Vollkorn, Avocados, Oliven*

Vitamine

organische Verbindungen, die keine Energieträger, sondern für lebenswichtige Funktionen notwendig sind. Vitamine kann der Körper (bis auf wenige Ausnahmen wie z. B. Vitamin D) nicht selbst herstellen und müssen mit der Nahrung aufgenommen werden.

Es gibt 9 wasserlösliche und 4 fettlösliche Vitamine. Vitamine sind wichtig für den Stoffwechsel, fungieren als Antioxidantien und sorgen für den Zellschutz.

Gute Vitamin-Lieferanten: *pflanzliche Ernährung mit viel frischem Obst und Gemüse wie z. B. Beeren, Äpfel, Zitrusfrüchte, grünes Blattgemüse, Paprika, Karotten, Tomaten, Sanddorn, Acerola*

Mineralstoffe und Spurenelemente

sind wichtig für fast alle Stoffwechselvorgänge (u. a. regelmäßigen Herzschlag, starke Knochen, gut funktionierendes Nervensystem) und können vom Körper nicht selbst hergestellt werden. Sie müssen mit der Nahrung aufgenommen werden. Die Unterteilung erfolgt in Mengenelemente, die der Körper in höheren Konzentrationen benötigt, wie z. B. Kalzium, Kali-

um, Natrium, Phosphor oder Magnesium, sowie in Spurenelemente, die man in kleineren Mengen benötigt, wie z. B. Eisen, Jod, Kupfer, Selen, Silicium, Zink oder Chrom.

Gute Mineralstoff-Lieferanten: *pflanzliche Ernährung mit viel frischem Obst und Gemüse wie z. B. grünes Blattgemüse, Bananen, Beeren, Gurken, Sellerie, Rote Bete, Nüsse*

Sekundäre Pflanzenstoffe

sind für die Pflanze und den Menschen von enormer Wichtigkeit. Sie können unter anderem den Blutdruck (Granatapfel) und das Cholesterin (durch Saponine) senken, den Blutzucker regulieren, die Verdauung fördern (Gewürze), Bakterien bekämpfen, das Immunsystem anregen, der Krebsentstehung vorbeugen (Carotinoide, Polyphenole u. a.), antioxidativ wirken oder hormonähnliche Wirkung (durch Phytoöstrogene) haben.

Wasser

Unser Körper besteht aus ca. 70 Prozent Wasser und ist auf die ständige Zufuhr der Flüssigkeit angewiesen, damit er optimal funktionieren kann. Ideal sind 1,5–2 Liter täglich – je nach Körpergewicht, Ernährung, Jahreszeit und Aktivität. Mit einer Ernährung, die aus sehr viel Rohkost besteht, deckt man schon einen Großteil des täglichen Flüssigkeitsbedarfs.

Sauerstoff

Sauerstoff gehört zu den wichtigsten Elementen. Wir nehmen ihn mit der Atemluft und mit der Nahrung auf.

Frisch gepresste Säfte können durch die Verarbeitung mit dem Entsafter schnell verdaut werden und liefern dem Körper in Minutenschnelle die darin enthaltenen Nährstoffe.

Wer profitiert von frischen Säften, Smoothies, Shots und Suppen?

Grundsätzlich sind frisch gepresste Obst- und Gemüsemischungen für alle Menschen sehr gut geeignet und von großem gesundheitlichen Nutzen, es sei denn, man hat Allergien oder Unverträglichkeiten gegenüber bestimmten Obst- und Gemüsesorten. Das sollte natürlich im Vorfeld abgeklärt sein.

Hervorragend eignen sich frisch gepresste Obst- und Gemüsemischungen für:

- gesundheitsbewusste Menschen, die sich ausgewogen ernähren möchten
- Kinder – insbesondere Schulkinder und Studenten, die sich gut konzentrieren müssen
- schwangere Frauen und stillende Mütter
- ältere Menschen mit Nährstoffdefiziten und schlechter Verdauung
- kranke Menschen und Menschen mit gesundheitlichen Problemen
- Menschen, die einen erhöhten Nährstoffbedarf haben (z. B. Sportler)
- Menschen, die entgiften und ihren Nährstoffhaushalt verbessern möchten
- Menschen, die sich nicht besonders gut ernähren und dies auf einfache Weise verbessern möchten

Frisch gepresste Obst- und Gemüsemischungen können vom Körper optimal und schnell verwertet werden. Daraus ergeben sich folgende Vorteile:

- leichte und schnelle Aufnahme von organischer, lebendiger Nahrung ohne Zusatz von Zucker, künstlichen Aromen, Konservierungs- und Farbstoffen (industriell gefertigte Säfte wurden hitzebehandelt)
- wenig Verdauungsarbeit für den Körper, da die Nährstoffe aus Obst und Gemüse innerhalb von Minuten ins Blut gelangen
- schwer verdauliche Fasern werden bei Obst- und Gemüsesäften entfernt
- geben dem Körper Energie und sorgen für Wohlbefinden
- Körper erhält reines, organisches Wasser
- man kann eine Vielzahl an Obst, Gemüse, Nüssen, Kräutern, Gräsern und Sprossen verwenden, die man so nicht essen würde
- schmecken köstlich und können dem eigenen Geschmack und den eigenen Vorlieben angepasst werden
- Slow Juicer und Kaltpress-Entsafter wirbeln nur sehr wenig Sauerstoff in die Säfte, Mixer und Zentrifugen jedoch aufgrund der hohen Umdrehungen sehr viel
- Mischungen mit viel Blattgrün sorgen für einen stabilen Blutzuckerspiegel, stellen uns pflanzliche Proteine zur Verfügung (z. B. Spinat) und transportieren Giftstoffe aus dem Körper
- Giftstoffe lagern sich gewöhnlich in den Fasern von Obst und Gemüse an und genau diese werden beim Entsaften extrahiert

Außerdem gönnen wir unserem Verdauungsapparat eine Pause, sodass er sich auf andere wichtige Dinge wie zum Beispiel das Reparieren von defekten Zellen konzentrieren kann. Wenn er die ganze Zeit mit der Verdauung von zum Beispiel fettiger und stärkehaltiger Nahrung beschäftigt ist, hat er nicht genügend Kapazität für Reparaturmaßnahmen.

Was können frisch gepresste Obst- und Gemüse-Mischungen bewirken?

Erzeugen im Körper ein basisches Milieu

Heutzutage werden viel zu viele Säuren konsumiert. Eigentlich sollte man 30 Prozent Säuren und 70 Prozent Basen aufnehmen. Die Realität sieht ganz anders aus. Es werden eher 30 Prozent Basen und 70 Prozent Säuren gegessen. Was sind säurebildende Lebensmittel? Alle tierischen Produkte, Kaffee, Limonaden, Fertigprodukte, Fast Food usw. Wenn jedoch mehr Basisches – also grüne Säfte, Smoothies, Suppen & Co. – konsumiert wird, gelangen jede Menge Basen in den Körper, welche die Säuren neutralisieren können.

Helfen bei der Entgiftung und beim Fasten

Zum Entgiften und Fasten eignen sich die Säfte, Smoothies, Suppen & Co. hervorragend, da sie Toxine aus dem Körper schaffen und die Leber bei der Entgiftung unterstützen. Gerade Weizengras, Algen, Zitronen, Kurkuma, Löwenzahn usw. sind hervorragend zur Unterstützung der Leber geeignet. Für eine Fastenkur sind die Säfte, Smoothies, Shots und Suppen gut kombinierbar, da sie – wie schon gesagt – wenig Verdauungsarbeit erfordern, aber auf der anderen Seite viele Nährstoffe bereitstellen. Man kann z. B. einmal pro Woche einen Safttag integrieren oder drei- bzw. fünftägige Saft- und Detoxkuren machen.

Auf der nächsten Seite geht´s weiter

Unterstützen beim Aufbau eines guten Immunsystems

Der Aufbau eines guten Immunsystems ist wichtig, um den Körper bestmöglich durch Eindringlinge von außen zu schützen. Wer ein starkes Immunsystem hat, kann jedem noch so schlimmen Angriff auf seine Zellen trotzen und diesen abwehren. Das Immunsystem kann man durch eine gute Ernährung, Sonnenlicht, guten Schlaf, wenig Stress, positive Gedanken, reines Wasser, Bewegung und viel frische Luft stärken. Auf all diese Punkte hat man großen Einfluss. Manchmal hat man das eine oder andere weniger gut im Griff, aber trotzdem kann oder sollte jeder so weit auf seinen Körper achten, dass die Rahmenbedingungen stimmen.

Säfte, Smoothies, Shots und Suppen sind dabei eine wichtige Säule, denn sie versorgen den Körper mit den lebenswichtigen Vitaminen A, B, C, E und K sowie Beta-Carotin, mit Mineralstoffen und Spurenelementen wie Magnesium, Zink, Eisen, Kupfer, Selen, Kieselsäure, Kalium, Kalzium usw.

Sind ideal zum Entschlacken und Abnehmen

Da Säfte, Smoothies, Shots und Suppen basenbildend sind, neutralisieren sie Säuren im Körper. Die Säuren sind oft mit Fett und Wasser in den Fettzellen eingelagert. Nimmt man nun mehr basenbildende Lebensmittel zu sich, kann man die Säuren leichter loswerden und damit auch das Fett und eingelagertes Wasser. Außerdem ersetzen gerade grüne Säfte oder Smoothies auf wunderbare Art und Weise den Kaffee oder Latte macchiato am Nachmittag. Kaffee sorgt meist nur für einen kurzen Energieanstieg. Bei grünen Säften und Smoothies steht hingegen nachhaltig Energie und Power zur Verfügung.

Als Vitaminbombe

Früchte in allen Farben des Regenbogens, wie gelbe Zitronen, Orangen, rote Beeren, tiefrote Blaubeeren, lila Brombeeren, Grünkohl und Wildkräuter liefern sehr viele Vitamine, die man in Form von Säften, Smoothies, Shots und Suppen konzentriert erhält – eine gute Möglichkeit, Defizite aufzufüllen.

Als Erfrischung und nach dem Sport zum Elektrolyt-Ausgleich

Wenn man schwitzt, verliert man über den Schweiß jede Menge Mineralien. Frisch gepresste Säfte sind daher eine ideale Möglichkeit, um diese auf natürliche Weise wieder aufzunehmen. Erfrischende Säfte nach dem Sport sind beispielsweise die Kombination aus Melone mit Minze sowie grüne Säfte mit Sellerie. Sellerie und Pfefferminze haben kühlende Eigenschaften, sodass der Körper auf natürliche Weise von innen abgekühlt wird.

Als Energiekick und Muntermacher

Da frisch gepresste Säfte eine sehr kurze Verdauungszeit von nur 10 bis 20 Minuten haben, versorgen sie unseren Körper rasant schnell mit Nährstoffen. Morgens sind sie daher ein toller Wachmacher und nachmittags holen sie einen – ganz ohne Koffein – aus dem berühmten Nachmittagstief heraus.

Als Muntermacher am Morgen eignen sich zum Beispiel warmes Wasser mit frisch gepresstem Zitronensaft und Ingwer oder auch alle Mischungen mit Obst. Am Nachmittag sind grüne Säfte mit frischer Pfefferminze sehr gut geeignet.

Beauty- und Anti-Aging-Elixiere

Schönheit lässt sich nicht einfach mit teurer Kosmetik herzaubern, aber Schönheit kann man durchaus essen beziehungsweise trinken. Wenn man sich nämlich richtig ernährt, kann man seine Vitalität, Gesundheit und damit auch seine Ausstrahlung steigern. Mineralien für die Schönheit sind beispielsweise Zink, Silizium, Magnesium und Schwefel und diese stecken in geballter Form in vielen Gemüsesorten wie grünem Blattgemüse und Wildkräutern. Auch Beeren, Granatapfel, Orange und Papaya liefern wertvolle Antioxidantien, die freie Radikale unschädlich machen. Nüsse, Mandeln, Kerne, Samen und Avocados wiederum stecken voller guter Fette. Somit können Säfte, Smoothies, Shots und Suppen einiges dafür tun, dass man so lange wie möglich seine Jugendlichkeit bewahrt.

Zur Förderung der Verdauung

Frisch gepresste Säfte können die Verdauung anregen. Früchte wirken beispielsweise am Morgen wie ein natürlicher Besen in den Verdauungsorganen. Gemüse hingegen ist eher aufbauend. Gerade grünes Blattgemüse enthält viel Magnesium und Kalium und fördert damit eine gute Verdauung, sorgt für ein gutes Nervensystem und wirkt ausgleichend.

Zur allgemeinen Balance

Säfte, Smoothies, Suppen und Shots mit viel grünem Blattgemüse sind richtige Konzentrate an Vitaminen und Mineralstoffen. Magnesium beruhigt beispielsweise das Nervensystem und wirkt daher ausgleichend auf den Organismus.

Als wärmender Saft im Winter

Verschiedene Zutaten wie Ingwer, Kurkuma, Pfeffer, Zimt und Chili können den Stoffwechsel auf Hochtouren bringen und im Körper wärmend wirken.

Gegen den Kater

Bloody Mary gibt es auch als gesunde Variante mit frischen Tomaten und Sellerie plus Pfeffer, Chili und Cayenne-Pfeffer. Dieser Saft lässt den Kater am nächsten Morgen schnell vergessen.

Obst und Gemüse als natürliches Anti-Aging-Mittel

Es gibt zwar keine Quelle der Jugend, aber man kann viel dafür tun, dass man so lange wie möglich seine Jugendlichkeit, Leistungsfähigkeit und Fitness erhält. Wichtige Faktoren hierfür sind: die Auswahl der richtigen Lebensmittel, ausreichendes Trinken von Wasser, Bewegung an frischer Luft, Tanken von Sonnenlicht, Entgiftungsmaßnahmen wie Massagen, Detox-Bäder und Sauna-Gänge.

Jeder hat es täglich selbst in der Hand, wie er seinen Körper ernährt und ob er ihm die für den Bau leistungsfähiger Zellen notwendigen Nährstoffe gibt, also im optimalen Fall fünf bis sieben Portionen Obst und Gemüse täglich.

Heute leiden viele Menschen an einem Mangel an Vitaminen, Mineralstoffen und Spurenelementen, denn oftmals enthält die Nahrung zu wenig sekundäre Pflanzenstoffe und Enzyme. Zum einen kann dies an einem geringen Konsum von Obst und Gemüse liegen, zum anderen beinhalten Früchte durch ausgelaugte Böden, Genmanipulationen, Züchtungen und gespritzte Felder einen geringeren Gehalt an Vitaminen und Mineralstoffen. Ein Mangel an Vitaminen, Mineralstoffen und Spurenelementen kann verschiedene unangenehme Folgen haben: brüchige Fingernägel, glanzlose Haare oder sogar Haarausfall, fahle Haut oder müde Augen. Mit frisch gepressten Säften, Smoothies, Shots und Suppen aus Obst, Gemüse, Kräutern, Gräsern und Sprossen lässt sich dieser Mangel an Vitalstoffen gut kompensieren. Bei der Auswahl der Zutaten ist es natürlich wichtig, möglichst frische und ungespritzte Ware zu verwenden. Auch saisonale Produkte beinhalten meist mehr Nährstoffe, da sie reif geerntet werden und kürzere Lagerzeiten haben. Mit Wildkräutern, die noch nie gentechnisch verändert wurden, lässt sich zudem ein Plus an Nährstoffen integrieren.

Viele Obst- & Gemüsesorten sind wahre Beauty-Lebensmittel und ein reichlicher Konsum von frischen Früchten kann daher die Haut schützen, reparieren und den Alterungsprozess verlangsamen.

Besondere Beauty-Lebensmittel im Focus

Versorgen die Haut mit viel Feuchtigkeit und lassen sie frisch, prall und strahlend wirken: *Wassermelone, Gurke, Aloe vera, Kokoswasser, Äpfel, Spinat, Wasser*

Regen die Kollagenproduktion der Haut an und sorgen für Festigkeit und Elastizität: *Granatapfel, Papaya, rotes Obst und Gemüse wie Erdbeeren, rote Äpfel, Kirschen, rote Paprika, Tomaten und Rote Bete, Zitrusfrüchte, Mango, Ananas*

Entzündungshemmende Eigenschaften und schnelle Heiler: *Aloe vera, Ingwer, Kurkuma, Zitrone, Spinat, Brokkoli, Zwiebeln, Knoblauch, Kirschen, Papaya, Blaubeeren*

Enthalten viele Fettsäuren für weiche und geschmeidige Haut: *Avocados, Nüsse, Öle wie z. B. Kokos- oder Olivenöl, Hanfsamen, Chiasamen*

Liefern viele Antioxidantien, schützen vor UV-Strahlung und beugen braunen Flecken vor: *Beeren, Kiwis, Bananen, Trauben, Kokosnuss, Mandeln, Rohschokolade, Zitrusfrüchte, Mango, Ananas, Sprossen, Kräuter*

Vitaminbomben für schöne, glänzende Haut: *Papaya, Beeren, Orangen, Kiwis, Paprika, Mandeln, Brokkoli, Karotten, Aroniabeere, Acerola, Hagebutte, Sanddorn*

Fülle an Mineralstoffen, die für die Zellbildung notwendig sind und die Haut strahlen lassen: *Feigen, grünes Blattgemüse, Kürbiskerne*

Welche Obst- und Gemüsesorten eignen sich für den Entsafter?

Ein Entsafter kann nahezu alle Obst- und Gemüsesorten, Kräuter, Wildkräuter, Gräser, Sprossen, Nüsse und Samen entsaften. Nur sehr weiche Sorten wie reife Avocados und Bananen lohnen sich weniger zum Pressen, können aber geschmacklich eine große Bereicherung sein. Diese eignen sich besser für die Verarbeitung im Mixer. Wer jedoch auf den herrlichen Geschmack von Avocados oder Bananen nicht verzichten möchte, kann sie durchaus mitpressen. Nur die Saft-Ausbeute lässt dabei ein wenig zu wünschen übrig. Generell erhält man den besten Saft aus frischen, knackigen Zutaten. Alte, schrumpelige Äpfel oder Karotten eignen sich nicht mehr zum Entsaften. Sie könnten eher zum Dörren verwendet werden.

Auch bei sehr harten Komponenten wie Avocadokernen, Mandeln, Nüssen wie Kokosnuss oder sehr trockenem Pressgut wie verschiedenen Gräsern kann ein Entsafter an seine Grenzen gelangen. Mandeln und Nüsse weicht man daher idealerweise vor dem Entsaften für einige Stunden in Wasser ein. Gräser und Wildkräuter presst man am besten in der Kombination mit feuchten Sorten wie Gurke, Apfel, Melone oder Ananas. Avocadokerne und Schalen der Kokosnuss gehören gar nicht in den Entsafter.

Pflanzliche Lebensmittel, die sich gut für den Entsafter eignen:
Zitrusfrüchte wie Orangen, Mandarinen, Grapefruits, Zitronen, Limetten, Äpfel, Birnen, Trauben, Maracuja, Kirschen, Granatapfel, Ananas, Wassermelone, Kiwi, Karotten, Rote Bete, Sellerie, Kohl, Salat, Spinat, Tomaten, Paprika, Gurken, Radieschen, Zucchini, Ingwer, Kurkuma, Sprossen, Sternfrucht, Aprikosen, Netzmelone, Papaya, Mango, Beeren, Gräser, Kräuter

Früchte, die weniger gut zum Entsaften geeignet sind:
Bananen, Avocados, überreife und sehr weiche Früchte, Fallobst

Ideal ist es, wenn man die Obst- und Gemüsesorten der Saison verarbeitet, denn diese Früchte werden in der Regel reif geerntet, haben kurze Lagerzeiten sowie Transportwege und daher einen hohen Nährstoffgehalt.

Tipps für Kauf, Reinigung, Verarbeitung und Lagerung von Obst, Gemüse, Gräsern und Kräutern

Für das Entsaften von Obst- und Gemüsemixturen verwendet man – wie schon erwähnt – die beste Qualität, die man bekommen kann. Denn: Je besser das Material, das man dem Körper zur Verfügung stellt, desto stärkere und widerstandsfähigere Zellen kann er aus der ihm zugeführten Nahrung bilden. Gespritztes Obst und Gemüse beinhalten sehr viele Pestizide und Herbizide. Damit kann der Körper nichts anfangen, es gibt keine Enzyme für diese Art von Chemikalien und der Körper möchte sie so schnell wie möglich wieder loswerden. Leider schafft er das nicht so gut und lagert es im Körper als Gift ab, gewöhnlich mit Wasser und Fett gepolstert in den Fettzellen. Also sollte man möglichst Bioware verwenden, Produkte vom Bauern des Vertrauens oder am idealsten aus dem Eigenanbau.

TIPP:

Wer konventionell angebautes Obst und Gemüse kauft, kann es mit Apfelessig waschen bzw. reinigen. Dazu gibt man in das Waschwasser (2–5 Liter) eine halbe Tasse Apfelessig und lässt die Früchte für etwa fünf Minuten darin liegen. Auch mit dem Wasser aus Wasserionisierern lassen sich diese Entgiftungsprozesse erzielen.

» VIDEO
Das 1x1 des Entsaftens

Tipps für den Entsafter

Tipps für die Verarbeitung von Obst, Gemüse und Kräutern mit dem Entsafter

- Granatapfel wird nur in grobe Stücke gebrochen, die weiße Haut beinhaltet wertvolle Bitterstoffe
- Beeren dürfen mit Blättern entsaftet werden, wie z. B. Erdbeeren, Himbeeren, Brombeeren
- Trauben werden mit Stiel verarbeitet
- Kräuter und Wildkräuter können mit Stiel verarbeitet werden; ideal im Wechsel mit feuchteren Sorten, da der Entsafter die Kräuter so leichter einziehen kann
- Tomaten: den Stiel entfernen; ganze Tomaten können zusammen mit dem Trester die Basis für eine Tomatensuppe, Gazpacho oder Pesto sein, vierteln
- Zitrusfrüchte: die Schale wird nur dünn entfernt, Kerne müssen nicht entfernt werden, vierteln. Bei Bioware kann die Schale von Zitrusfrüchten mit verarbeitet werden.
- Kernobst: bei Äpfeln und Birnen kann das Gehäuse je nach Belieben und Geschmack verarbeitet werden, vierteln
- Steinobst: bei Kirschen, Pflaumen und Aprikosen muss der harte Kern entfernt werden, vierteln oder halbieren
- Karotten, Rote Bete, Wassermelonen, Ingwer und Kurkuma können problemlos mit Schale entsaftet werden, vorher die Schale mit einer Gemüsebürste gut abschrubben. Von Karotten und Roter Bete kann auch das Grün mit entsaftet werden
- Ananas: Schale und Strunk entfernen, in grobe Stücke schneiden
- Mango, Avocado: Schale und Kern entfernen, vierteln
- Papaya: Schale und Kerne entfernen, ein paar Kerne können auch mit entsaftet werden und sorgen für schärfere Mischungen
- Maracujas werden in der Mitte durchgeschnitten und das Fruchtfleisch aus der Frucht gelöffelt
- Paprika: Stiel und Kerne entfernen, in grobe Stücke schneiden
- Gurken in grobe Stücke schneiden
- Nüsse und Mandeln: für mindestens vier Stunden in Wasser einweichen, danach bei Bedarf nochmals spülen
- Karotten: unbedingt ein wenig Kokos- oder Olivenöl dazugeben, damit die fettlöslichen Vitamine wie Beta-Carotin vom Körper besser aufgenommen werden können

Tipps für das Reinigen und Vorbereiten von Obst, Gemüse und Kräutern zum Entsaften

- Obst und Gemüse unter fließendem Wasser und erst kurz vor dem Entsaften reinigen.
- Mit einer kleinen Bürste können Sand und Erde gut entfernt werden.
- Bei Bioware bitte immer mit Schale pressen, da gerade in der Schale besonders viele Nährstoffe stecken (außer bei Avocados, Papaya, Ananas, Mango, Maracuja, Banane und Zitrusfrüchten).
- Obst und Gemüse möglichst schnell verarbeiten, dadurch bleiben die meisten Nährstoffe erhalten.
- Faule Stellen immer ausschneiden bzw. entfernen.
- Nüsse idealerweise vor dem Entsaften für ca. 4 Stunden in Wasser einweichen, da sie dadurch besser verdaut werden können.
- Große und harte Kerne z. B. von Mangos, Avocados, Pflaumen und Kirschen vor dem Entsaften entfernen. Kerne von Wassermelonen, Trauben, Beeren, Äpfeln und Birnen können mitgepresst werden.

Tipps für die richtige Lagerung von Obst und Gemüse

Wie und wo lagere ich Tomaten, Äpfel, Gurken und Salat am besten? Im Kühlschrank, im Keller, in der Speisekammer oder in der Obstschale? Wie bleiben die einzelnen Sorten am längsten frisch?

- Generell werden die meisten Obst- und Gemüsesorten am besten dunkel, kühl und bei hoher Luftfeuchtigkeit gelagert, denn niedrige Temperaturen verlängern die Haltbarkeit. Also ist man mit dem Gemüsefach im Kühlschrank ganz gut bedient, da die Temperaturen dort zwischen 5 und 8 Grad liegen. Allerdings sind die optimalen Lagerbedingungen von Sorte zu Sorte ganz unterschiedlich.
- Südfrüchte sollten gar nicht im Kühlschrank gelagert werden. Bananen verlieren beispielsweise bei niedrigen Temperaturen deutlich

ENTSAFTER	MIXER
Langsame und schonende Verarbeitung von Obst und Gemüse zu Säften (Entsafter arbeiten mit ca. 50 Umdrehungen in der Minute)	Verarbeitung von Obst und Gemüse mit hoher Umdrehungszahl zu Smoothies (ca. 10000 bis 30000 Umdrehungen in der Minute)
Entsafter extrahieren Nährstoffe und Wasser, Fasern werden abgetrennt – dünne Konsistenz	Verarbeitung und Konsum der gesamten Fruchtanteile – dicke Konsistenz
Schnelle Verdauung, Nährstoffe gelangen in rund 20 Minuten ins Blut = Express-Variante, um Nährstoffe aufzunehmen	Verdauungszeit wie bei ganzen Früchten, ca. 3 Stunden = Fasern verlangsamen den Verdauungsprozess und geben Nährstoffe kontinuierlich ins Blut ab
Ein Glas Saft entspricht ca. 3 Portionen Obst und Gemüse	Ein Glas Smoothie entspricht ca. 1 Portion Obst und Gemüse
Aufnahmerate an Nährstoffen in Form von Säften bis zu vier Mal höher als in Form von ganzen Früchten	Mixprozess schließt die Fasern auf, sodass die Früchte bzw. Gemüse besser verdaut werden können als durch kurzes Kauen
Durch die Verwendung von viel Obst kann Blutzucker schneller ansteigen, besser: süße Früchte maßvoll verwenden und mehr grünes Blattgemüse mitpressen	Nährstoffe gelangen kontinuierlich und langsam in die Blutbahn. Ein schneller Anstieg des Blutzuckers wird damit verhindert
Säfte sind rasch verdaut und man bekommt danach schneller wieder Hunger	Smoothies sind sättigend und ideal als Ersatz für Frühstück oder Zwischenmahlzeit
Säfte, die mit Slow Juicers hergestellt werden, oxidieren nicht so schnell	Oxidierung durch Einwirbelung von Sauerstoff und hohe Umdrehungszahl
Säfte sollten langsam getrunken und nicht als Durstlöcher verwendet werden	Smoothies sollten immer gut eingespeichelt und am besten wie eine Suppe gelöffelt werden
Schnelle Zubereitung, etwas mehr Reinigungsaufwand als beim Mixer	Schnelle Zubereitung, etwas weniger Reinigungsaufwand als beim Entsafter
Säfte lassen sich länger aufbewahren als Smoothies	Smoothies sollten am besten gleich nach dem Mixen getrunken werden
Entsafter, vor allem langsam drehende Slow Juicer, arbeiten sehr leise	Mixer, Thermomix und Pürierstab arbeiten aufgrund der hohen Umdrehungszahl meist sehr lautstark

Saisonkalender

JANUAR

Freiland: Chicorée, Feldsalat, Grünkohl, Lauch/Porree, Pastinaken, Portulak, Rosenkohl, Schwarzwurzeln, Steckrüben, Wirsing
Gewächshaus: Champignons, Feldsalat, Rauke, Sellerie, Spinat
Lagerware: Äpfel, Birnen, Chinakohl, Kartoffeln, Kürbis, Möhren, Pastinaken, Radicchio, Rote Bete, Rotkohl, Schwarzer Winterrettich, Stauden-Sellerie, Weiß- und Spitzkohl, Zwiebeln

FEBRUAR

Freiland: Chicorée, Feldsalat, Grünkohl, Porree/Lauch, Pastinaken, Portulak, Rosenkohl, Schwarzwurzeln, Wirsing
Gewächshaus: Champignons, Feldsalat, Rauke, Sellerie, Spinat
Lagerware: Äpfel, Chinakohl, Kartoffeln, Kürbis, Möhren, Pastinaken, Radicchio, Rote Bete, Rotkohl, Schwarzer Winterrettich, Schwarzwurzeln, Stauden-Sellerie, Steckrüben, Weiß- und Spitzkohl, Zwiebeln

MÄRZ

Freiland: Chicorée, Feldsalat, Spinat, Porree/Lauch, Pastinaken, Portulak, Rosenkohl
Gewächshaus: Champignons, Feldsalat, Kopfsalat, Radieschen, Rauke, Rhabarber, Sellerie
Lagerware: Äpfel, Chinakohl, Kartoffeln, Kürbis, Möhren, Rote Bete, Rotkohl, Schwarzer Winterrettich, Schwarzwurzeln, Stauden-Sellerie, Weiß- und Spitzkohl, Wirsing, Zwiebeln

APRIL

Freiland: Chicorée, Feldsalat, Rhabarber, Morcheln, Portulak, Rauke, Spargel, Spinat
Gewächshaus: Blumenkohl, Champignons, Feldsalat, Frühlingszwiebeln, Kohlrabi, Kopfsalat, Mangold, Radieschen, Rauke, Sellerieknollen
Lagerware: Äpfel, Kartoffeln, Kürbis, Möhren, Pastinaken, Rote Bete, Rotkohl, Schwarzer Winterrettich, Stauden-Sellerie, Weiß- und Spitzkohl, Wirsing, Zwiebeln

MAI

Freiland: Batavia, Eichblattsalat, Endiviensalat, Feldsalat, Frühlingszwiebeln, Kohlrabi, Kopfsalat, Lollo rot/grün, Mangold, Morcheln, Radieschen, Rauke, Rhabarber, Spargel, Spinat, Spitzkohl, Wirsing
Gewächshaus: Auberginen, Blumenkohl, Champignons, Chinakohl, Eissalat, Endiviensalat, Erdbeeren, Fenchel, Kohlrabi, Kopfsalat, Mairüben, Möhren, Romanasalat, Salatgurken, Stauden-Sellerie, Tomaten
Lagerware: Äpfel, Kartoffeln, Möhren, Rotkohl, Weiß- und Spitzkohl, Zwiebeln

JUNI

Freiland: Batavia, Blumenkohl, Brokkoli, dicke Bohnen, Eichblattsalat, Eisbergsalat, Endiviensalat, Erbsen, Erdbeeren, Feldsalat, Frühlingszwiebeln, Johannisbeeren, Kirschen, Kartoffeln, Kohlrabi, Kopfsalat, Porree/Lauch, Lollo rot/grün, Mairüben, Mangold, Möhren, Pfifferlinge, Radicchio, Radieschen, Rauke, Rhabarber, Romanasalat, Rotkohl, Salatgurke, Spargel, Busch- und Stangenbohnen, Spitz- und Weißkohl, Stachelbeeren, Wirsing, Zwiebeln
Gewächshaus: Auberginen, Champignons, Chinakohl, Fenchel, Himbeeren, Paprika, Salatgurken, Stauden-Sellerie, Tomaten

JULI

Freiland: Aprikosen, Batavia, Blumenkohl, Brokkoli, Brombeeren, dicke Bohnen, Eichblattsalat, Einlegegurken, Eisbergsalat, Endiviensalat, Erbsen, Erdbeeren, Feldsalat, Frühlingszwiebeln, Heidelbeeren, Himbeeren, Johannisbeeren, Kartoffeln, Kirschen, Kohlrabi, Kopfsalat, Porree/Lauch, Lollo rot/grün, Mairüben, Mangold, Mirabellen, Möhren, Pfifferlinge, Pfirsiche, Pflaumen, Portulak, Radicchio, Radieschen, Rauke, Rettich, Romanasalat, Rotkohl, Salatgurken, Stachelbeeren,

Busch- und Stangenbohnen, Stauden-Sellerie, Tomaten, Weißkohl, Wirsing, Zucchini, Zwetschgen, Zwiebeln

AUGUST

Freiland: Äpfel, Aprikosen, Auberginen, Batavia, Birnen, Blumenkohl, Brokkoli, Brombeeren, Chinakohl, Dicke Bohnen, Eichblattsalat, Einlegegurken, Eisbergsalat, Endiviensalat, Erbsen, Erdbeeren, Feldsalat, Frühlingszwiebeln, Heidelbeeren, Himbeeren, Johannisbeeren, Kartoffeln, Kirschen, Kohlrabi, Kopfsalat, Kürbis, Porree/Lauch, Lollo rot/grün, Mairüben, Mangold, Mirabellen, Möhren, Paprika, Pastinaken, Pfifferlinge, Pfirsiche, Pflaumen, Portulak, Radicchio, Radieschen, Rauke, Rettich, Romanasalat, Rotkohl, Salatgurken, Stachelbeeren, Stangenbohnen, Stauden-Sellerie, Trauben, Tomaten, Wassermelonen, Weißkohl, Wirsing, Zucchini, Zuckermais, Zwetschgen, Zwiebeln

SEPTEMBER

Freiland: Äpfel, Auberginen, Batavia, Birnen, Blumenkohl, Brokkoli, Brombeeren, Chinakohl, Eichblattsalat, Einlegegurken, Eisbergsalat, Endiviensalat, Erdbeeren, Feldsalat, Fenchel, Frühlingszwiebeln, Heidelbeeren, Holunderbeeren, Kartoffeln, Kohlrabi, Kopfsalat, Kürbis, Porree/Lauch, Lollo rot/grün, Mairüben, Mangold, Meerrettich, Mirabellen, Möhren, Paprika, Pastinaken, Pfifferlinge, Pflaumen, Portulak, Quitten, Radicchio, Radieschen, Rauke, Rettich, Romanasalat, Rote Bete, Rotkohl, Salatgurken, Sellerie, Spinat, Stachelbeeren, Stangenbohnen, Stauden-Sellerie, Trauben, Tomaten, Wassermelonen, Weißkohl, Wirsing, Zucchini, Zuckermais, Zwetschgen, Zwiebeln

OKTOBER

Freiland: Äpfel, Birnen, Blumenkohl, Brokkoli, Brombeeren, Chicorée, Chinakohl, Eichblattsalat, Einlegegurken, Eisbergsalat, Endiviensalat, Feldsalat, Fenchel, Frühlingszwiebeln, Holunderbeeren, Kartoffeln, Kohlrabi, Kopfsalat, Kürbis, Porree/Lauch, Lollo rot/grün, Mairüben, Meerrettich, Möhren, Paprika, Pastinaken, Pfifferlinge, Portulak, Quitten, Radicchio, Radieschen, Rauke, Romanasalat, Rosenkohl, Rote Bete, Rotkohl, Schwarzer Winterrettich, Schwarzwurzel, Sellerie, Spinat, Stangenbohnen, Stauden-Sellerie, Steckrüben, Trauben, Tomaten, Weißkohl, Wirsing, Zucchini, Zuckermais, Zwetschgen, Zwiebeln

NOVEMBER

Freiland: Chicorée, Chinakohl, Endiviensalat, Feldsalat, Frühlingszwiebeln, Grünkohl, Kürbis, Lauch, Mairüben, Meerrettich, Pastinaken, Pfifferlinge, Portulak, Quitten, Radicchio, Romanasalat, Rosenkohl, Rote Bete, Rotkohl, Schwarzwurzeln, Sellerie, Steckrüben, Wirsing, Weißkohl
Gewächshaus: Champignons, Kohlrabi, Kopfsalat, Paprika, Radieschen, Rauke, Spinat, Stauden-Sellerie
Lagerware: Äpfel, Birnen, Kartoffeln, Kürbis, Möhren, Pastinaken, Schwarzer Winterrettich, Zucchini, Zuckermais, Zwiebeln

DEZEMBER

Freiland: Chicorée, Endiviensalat, Feldsalat, Grünkohl, Lauch, Pastinaken, Rosenkohl, Schwarzwurzeln, Steckrüben, Wirsing
Gewächshaus: Champignons, Feldsalat, Kohlrabi, Rauke, Sellerie, Spinat, Stauden-Sellerie
Lagerware: Äpfel, Birnen, Kartoffeln, Kürbis, Möhren, Pastinaken, Radicchio, Rote Bete, Rotkohl, Schwarzer Winterrettich, Stauden-Sellerie, Wirsing, Weißkohl, Zwiebeln

Booster

für Säfte, Smoothies, Shots und Suppen

Der Nährstoffgehalt von frisch gepressten Säften, Smoothies, Shots und Suppen kann mit Gewürzen, Samen, Kräutern und Pulvern noch weiter erhöht werden. Dadurch lassen sich auch bestimmte Wirkungen erzielen oder verstärken wie z. B. die Entgiftung ankurbeln, die Verdauung anregen, beruhigen, energetisieren, wärmen oder einen schnellen Blutzuckeranstieg verhindern. Sogenannte Booster kann man in den Saft einrühren oder ihn damit verzieren.

TIPP

Bei Säften mit Möhren oder Früchten, die viel Beta-Karotin enthalten, sollte man immer etwas Kokos- oder Olivenöl hinzufügen, da fettlösliche Vitamine wie Beta-Karotin besser aufgenommen werden können.

Bei Wildkräutern ist es ratsam, zunächst kleine Mengen zu verwenden und diese dann langsam zu steigern. Wildkräuter wie z. B. Löwenzahn oder Brennnessel haben entgiftende Wirkung und könnten den Körper daher anfangs belasten. Daher sollte man ihn langsam an Wildkräuter gewöhnen. Empfehlenswerte Mengen für den Anfang sind beispielsweise drei bis vier Blätter Löwenzahn oder Himbeerblätter oder ein bis zwei Stängel Brennnessel. Größere Mengen können vor allem am Abend zu Unruhe führen.

» VIDEO
Booster

Booster

PULVER: Chlorella, Spirulina, Gerstengras, Weizengras, Brennnessel, Rote Bete, Moringa

GEWÜRZE: Meer- oder Steinsalz, Pfeffer, Paprika, Cayenne-Pfeffer, Kurkuma, Ingwer, Chili, Zimt

BLÄTTER: Brombeere, Himbeere, Frauenmantel, Grünes von Möhren und Roter Bete

WILDKRÄUTER: Brennnessel, Löwenzahn, Giersch, Gänseblümchen, Klee, Gundermann, Spitzwegerich, Brunnenkresse, Sauerampfer, Dost, Vogelmiere

KÜCHENKRÄUTER: Petersilie, Schnittlauch, Minze, Basilikum, Thymian, Zitronenmelisse, Oregano, Koriander, Rosmarin, Lavendel, Salbei

BLÜTEN: Lavendel, Kapuzinerkresse, Schnittlauchblüten, Rotkleeblüten, Gänseblümchen, Hibiskus

SAMEN UND NÜSSE: Hanfsamen, Chiasamen, Leinsamen, Lupinensamen, gemahlene Nüsse und Mandeln

SONSTIGES: Kokosraspeln, Sprossen, Holunderbeeren

Weiterverwendung des Tresters

Wenn man regelmäßig frisch gepresste Obst- und Gemüsemischungen herstellt, bleibt auch jede Menge Trester übrig. Was kann man damit tun?

Der Trester muss nicht unbedingt im Müll landen. Es gibt einige Möglichkeiten, ihn sinnvoll weiterzuverarbeiten. Nachfolgend finden sich einige Anregungen:

Verwenden

- zum Andicken von Suppen oder Smoothies
- als Zusatz für Soßen wie Gemüsesuppen, Nudelsoßen oder Currys
- als Basis und Geschmacksträger für Veggie-Burger
- als Zusatz für Backwaren wie Muffins, Kuchen, Brot oder Plätzchen
- zum Dörren mit Nüssen, Samen und getrockneten Früchten (Müsliriegel)
- als Basis für pikante Dips und Aufstriche
- für Rohkost-Salate
- als Zusatz für Pfannkuchen und Omeletts
- für Hautmasken
- als Zusatz zum Tierfutter

» VIDEO
Ideen für Weiterverwendung des Tresters

Der Trester von Sellerie, Brokkoli, Möhren, Kohl, Fenchel, Petersilie und Spinat eignet sich wunderbar für gekochte Gerichte.

Der Trester von Obst wie Äpfeln, Pfirsichen, Beeren, Orangen, Roter Bete oder Birnen ist ein ideales Süßungsmittel.

Außerdem lässt sich der Trester auch gut als natürlicher Dünger in die Gartenerde einarbeiten.

TIPP
Säfte, Smoothies, Shots und Suppen sollten immer in Gläsern aufbewahrt werden, da diese geschmacksneutral sind.

Haltbarkeit

von Säften, Smoothies, Shots und Suppen

Frisch gepresste Säfte, Smoothies, Power-Shots und Suppen sollten idealerweise sofort nach dem Pressen getrunken bzw. gegessen werden, denn dann sind die meisten Nährstoffe enthalten. Man hat jedoch nicht immer die Möglichkeit, frisch zu pressen. Daher kann man Säfte, Shots, Smoothies und die Basis für Suppen auch auf Vorrat produzieren. Sie lassen sich problemlos bis zu zwei Tage im Kühlschrank aufbewahren. Damit sie auch noch am nächsten Tag farblich schön aussehen, sollte man dazu immer etwas Zitronensaft mitpressen, da Zitronensaft wie ein natürliches Konservierungsmittel wirkt.

Die tägliche Ration

Zwei Gläser frisch gepresster Saft sind die ideale Menge, um den Tagesbedarf an Vitaminen, Mineralstoffen und Spurenelementen zu decken. Bei therapeutischen Anwendungen, zur Entgiftung oder zum Fasten sind jedoch ein bis zwei Liter täglich empfehlenswert.

Wer zum Beispiel seinen Nährstoffhaushalt schnell auffüllen möchte, kann täglich mehrere Gläser Säfte oder dementsprechend Smoothies und Shots trinken bzw. Suppen essen. Hierbei sollte man jedoch darauf achten, nicht viele reine Obstsäfte zu trinken und grünes Blattgemüse zu variieren. Es ist nicht ratsam, jeden Tag Säfte, Smoothies oder Shots mit Grünkohl oder Blattspinat zu trinken, sondern man sollte die grünen Bestandteile abwechseln.

So sieht ein Saft- bzw. Detoxtag aus

» VIDEO
Tipps für Saftfasten

1

Morgens
1 Glas Zitronen-wasser oder Kurkuma-Tonic

2

Vormittags
1 Glas Saft, z. B. mit Apfel, Orange, Roter Bete und Ingwer

3

Mittags
1 Glas Saft, 1 Smoothie oder 1 Suppe nach Belieben

4

Nachmittags
1 Glas Grüner Saft nach Belieben

6

Abends
1 Glas Saft, 1 Smoothie oder 1 Suppe nach Belieben

Säfte

SÄFTE

Gesund & exotisch

Zutaten für 2 Gläser Saft

- *2 Äpfel*
- *2 Orangen*
- *2 Möhren*
- *½ Rote Bete*
- *1 Maracuja*

Zubereitung

Die Äpfel waschen, vierteln und nach Belieben das Kerngehäuse entfernen oder belassen. Die Orangen schälen und ebenfalls vierteln. Möhren und Rote Bete waschen. Möhren in grobe Streifen, Rote Bete in Stücke schneiden. Alles in den Entsafter geben.
Die Maracuja aufschneiden, mit dem Löffel das Maracuja-Fleisch auslöffeln und ebenfalls in den Entsafter geben.

TIPP

Die Maracuja sollte von außen schon leicht verschrumpelt aussehen. Dann sind Reifegrad und Aroma der Frucht ideal.
Bei Säften mit Möhren empfiehlt es sich, ein paar Tropfen Olivenöl dazuzugeben, weil dadurch die fettlöslichen Vitamine wie Beta-Carotin vom Körper besser aufgenommen werden können.

NUTZEN

— Stärkung des Immunsystems
— Vitaminbombe
— Energiekick

Küchengerät: 

Jugend-Elixier

Zutaten für 2 Gläser Saft

› *150 g Erdbeeren*
› *150 g Himbeeren*
› *150 g Blaubeeren*
› *250 g Trauben*
› *1 Granatapfel*

Zubereitung

Die Erdbeeren, Himbeeren, Blaubeeren und Trauben waschen. Die Kerne aus dem Granatapfel lösen. Alle Zutaten nacheinander in den Entsafter geben.

TIPP

Bevor man den Granatapfel entkernt, ist es hilfreich, ihn auf der Arbeitsplatte mit leichtem Druck hin und her zu rollen. Die Kerne können danach leicht mit einem Löffel herausgeklopft werden. Stiele und Kerne der Trauben müssen beim Entsaften nicht entfernt werden.

NUTZEN

— Energiekick
— Stärkung des Immunsystems
— Vitaminbombe
— Anti-Aging
— Beauty-Elixier – für einen schönen Teint

Beauty-Drink

Zutaten für 2 Gläser Saft

› *2 Grapefruits*
› *2 kleine Papayas*
› *4 Aprikosen*
› *200 g Kirschen*

Zubereitung

Die Grapefruits schälen und vierteln. Von der Papaya die Schale ablösen und die Kerne entfernen. Das Fruchtfleisch in grobe Stücke schneiden. Die Aprikosen und Kirschen waschen und entkernen. Alle Zutaten in den Entsafter geben.

TIPP

Der Trester dieses gepressten Saftes lässt sich gut weiterverarbeiten und eignet sich zum Beispiel auch als Gesichtsmaske.

NUTZEN

— Anti-Aging
— Beauty-Elixier
— Stärkung des Immunsystems
— Vitaminbombe

 Küchengerät für beide Rezepte: 

JUGEND-ELIXIER

BEAUTY-DRINK

SOMMERFRISCHE

SWEET GREENS

Sommerfrische

Zutaten für 2 Gläser Saft

- *150 g Erdbeeren*
- *2 Pfirsiche*
- *1 Stängel Minze*
- *¼ Melone*

Zubereitung

Erdbeeren, Pfirsiche und Minze waschen. Den Kern der Pfirsiche entfernen und Pfirsiche vierteln. Das Fruchtfleisch aus der Melone lösen und die Melone in grobe Stücke schneiden. Alle Zutaten in den Entsafter geben.

VARIATION

Mit dem Saft einer halben Limette schmeckt der Saft noch aromatischer und weniger süß.

NUTZEN

— Energiekick und Erfrischung
— ideal nach dem Sport
— Muntermacher
— ideal fürs Abnehmen und Fasten
— zur Entgiftung

Sweet Greens

Zutaten für 2 Gläser Saft

- *300 g Trauben*
- *100 g Spinat*
- *1 Stängel Basilikum*
- *½ Limette*
- *½ Ananas*

Zubereitung

Die Trauben, den Spinat und das Basilikum waschen. Von der Limette die Schale entfernen, die Frucht vierteln. Von der Ananas ebenfalls die Schale entfernen und die Frucht in grobe Stücke schneiden. Alle Zutaten in den Entsafter geben.

VARIATION

Anstatt Trauben zu verwenden, kann man auch 2 Orangen pressen.

NUTZEN

— Stärkung des Immunsystems
— Vitaminbombe
— Anti-Aging
— Beauty-Elixier
— Förderung der Verdauung
— ideal zum Abnehmen und Fasten

Küchengerät für beide Rezepte: 

Tiefgrün

Zutaten für 2 Gläser Saft

- *2 Blätter Mangold (alternativ Grünkohl oder 3 Stängel Sellerie)*
- *100 g Spinat*
- *½ Gurke*
- *1 Stängel Minze*
- *2 Orangen*
- *½ Zitrone*

Zubereitung

Mangold, Spinat, Gurke und Minze waschen. Den Mangold in Streifen, die Gurke in Stücke schneiden. Von den Orangen und der Zitrone die Schale entfernen und beide Früchte vierteln. Alle Zutaten in den Entsafter geben.

TIPP

Zu diesem Saft passen auch Ingwer und Kurkuma sehr gut.

VARIANTE FÜR DIABETIKER

Anstatt der 2 Orangen 3 grüne Äpfel verwenden.

NUTZEN

— Erfrischung
— Stärkung des Immunsystems
— Vitaminbombe
— Anti-Aging
— Beauty-Elixier
— ideal fürs Abnehmen und Fasten
— reinigend

 Küchengerät: 

Mineralienpower

Zutaten für 2 Gläser Saft

- *4 mittelgroße Tomaten*
- *2 Stangen Sellerie*
- *1 roter oder gelber Paprika*
- *½ Rote Bete*
- *3 Möhren*
- *1 Stängel Petersilie*
- *je 1 Prise Pfeffer und Himalaya-Salz*

Zubereitung

Tomaten, Sellerie, Paprika, Rote Bete, Möhren und Petersilie waschen. Die Tomaten vierteln, den Sellerie halbieren und in grobe Stücke schneiden, Paprika in Streifen schneiden und die Rote Bete vierteln. Alle Zutaten in den Entsafter geben. Abschließend im Glas den Saft nach Belieben mit Pfeffer und Salz würzen.

TIPP

Säfte können auch auf Vorrat gepresst werden und sind problemlos 2 Tage in Glasflaschen im Kühlschrank haltbar. Als natürliches Konservierungsmittel gibt man Zitronen- oder Limettensaft dazu.

NUTZEN

— Energiekick
— Stärkung des Immunsystems
— Vitaminbombe
— verdauungsfördernd
— ideal fürs Abnehmen
— für Diabetiker geeignet
— schneller Elektrolyt-Ausgleich

Küchengerät: 

Winterfit

Zutaten für 2 Gläser Saft

- *2 Orangen (oder 4 Mandarinen)*
- *½ Ananas*
- *1 kleine Zitrone*
- *4 cm Kurkuma*
- *3 cm Ingwer*

Zubereitung

Von den Orangen, der Ananas und der Zitrone die Schale entfernen. Die Orangen und Zitrone vierteln. Die Ananas in grobe Stücke schneiden. Kurkuma und Ingwer waschen. Alle Zutaten in den Entsafter geben.

TIPP

Wer den Geschmack mag, kann je nach Belieben mehr Kurkuma und Ingwer verwenden.

NUTZEN

— Stärkung des Immunsystems
— Vitaminbombe
— ideal fürs Abnehmen und Fasten
— zur Entgiftung
— regt den Stoffwechsel an

Küchengerät: 

Hallo wach!

Zutaten für 2 Gläser Saft

- *2 Äpfel*
- *½ Ananas*
- *300 g Weizengras*

Zubereitung

Die Äpfel waschen, vierteln und bei Bedarf das Kerngehäuse entfernen. Von der Ananas die Schale entfernen und die Frucht in grobe Stücke schneiden. Das Weizengras waschen und in 4 cm lange Stücke schneiden. Alle Zutaten in den Entsafter geben.

TIPP

Das Aroma der Säfte lässt sich mit Kräutern wie Minze, Zitronenmelisse, Basilikum und Petersilie verfeinern und intensivieren.

VARIANTE FÜR DIABETIKER

Anstatt mit Ananas das Weizengras nur mit grünen Äpfeln pressen.

NUTZEN

- Energiekick
- Muntermacher
- ideal fürs Abnehmen und Fasten
- zur Entgiftung
- Stärkung des Immunsystems
- Vitaminbombe
- verdauungsfördernd

» **VIDEO**
Verarbeitung von Weizengras – Von der Aussaat bis zum Saft

Küchengerät:

Detox intensiv

Zutaten für 2 Gläser Saft

- *2 Äpfel*
- *300 g Trauben*
- *2 Kapseln Aktivkohle*
- *200 g Kirschen*

Zubereitung

Die Äpfel waschen, vierteln und bei Bedarf das Kerngehäuse entfernen. Die Trauben und Kirschen waschen. Die Kirschen entkernen. Äpfel, Trauben und Kirschen in den Entsafter geben. Danach die Kapseln mit Aktivkohle öffnen und in den fertigen Saft einrühren.

TIPP

Aktivkohle ist als Pulver und in Kapselform erhältlich. Sie eignet sich auch zur Zahn-Aufhellung.

NUTZEN

- wirkt entgiftend
- ideal zum Abnehmen und Fasten
- Stärkung des Immunsystems

Küchengerät: 

Paradies im Glas

Zutaten für 2 Gläser Saft

› *½ Ananas*
› *1 Granatapfel*
› *2 Orangen*

Zubereitung

Von der Ananas die Schale entfernen und die Frucht in grobe Stücke schneiden. Den Granatapfel entkernen. Von den Orangen die Schale entfernen und vierteln. Alle Zutaten in den Entsafter geben.

TIPP

Um die Fruchtsüße abzumildern, kann eine Zitrone oder Limette mitgepresst werden.

NUTZEN

— Stärkung des Immunsystems
— Vitaminbombe
— Anti-Aging
— Beauty-Elixier

Küchengerät: 

KOKOS KÜSST BEERE

SUMMER COOLER

Kokos küsst Beere

Zutaten für 2 Gläser Saft

- *200 g Erdbeeren*
- *200 g Himbeeren*
- *1 Glas Kokoswasser*

Zubereitung

Die Erdbeeren und Himbeeren waschen und gemeinsam mit dem Kokoswasser in den Entsafter geben.

TIPP

Hierfür kann man auch einen bunten Beerenmix mit zusätzlichen Brombeeren und Heidelbeeren verwenden.

NUTZEN

— Stärkung des Immunsystems
— Vitaminbombe
— Energiekick
— Anti-Aging
— Beauty-Elixier

Summer Cooler

Zutaten für 2 Gläser Saft

- *250 g Erdbeeren*
- *¼ Wassermelone*
- *2 Stängel Minze*
- *½ Zitrone*

Zubereitung

Erdbeeren und Minze waschen. Aus der Melone das Fruchtfleisch herauslösen. Von der Zitrone die Schale entfernen und die Frucht vierteln. Danach alles in den Entsafter geben.

NUTZEN

— Erfrischung
— Stärkung des Immunsystems
— Vitaminbombe
— Energiekick
— Anti-Aging
— Beauty-Elixier

Küchengerät für beide Rezepte: 

Erfrischung im Herbst

Zutaten für 2 Gläser Saft

› *2 Birnen*
› *2 Äpfel*
› *300 g Trauben*
› *1 Stängel Minze*

Zubereitung

Birnen und Äpfel waschen, vierteln und bei Bedarf das Kerngehäuse entfernen. Die Trauben und Minze ebenfalls waschen. Alle Zutaten in den Entsafter geben.

TIPP

Trauben können auch am Stiel in den Entsafter wandern. Allerdings sollte man darauf achten, dass die Stiele nicht zu lang und zu dick sind.

NUTZEN

— Stärkung des Immunsystems
— Vitaminbombe
— Energiekick
— Förderung der Verdauung
— ideal zum Abnehmen und Fasten

 Küchengerät: 

Lebkuchen-Drink

Zutaten für 2 Gläser Saft

- *200 g Mandeln*
- *100 g Haselnüsse*
- *1 Orange*
- *½ Zitrone*
- *2 Äpfel*
- *2 EL Honig*
- *1 Prise Zimt*
- *1 Prise Lebkuchengewürz*
- *1 Prise Kakaopulver*

Zubereitung

Die Mandeln und Haselnüsse für mindestens 4 Stunden in Wasser einweichen. Danach das Wasser abgießen und die Mandeln und Nüsse spülen. Von der Orange und Zitrone die Schale abschneiden und die Früchte vierteln. Äpfel waschen, bei Bedarf das Kerngehäuse entfernen und die Äpfel vierteln. Mandeln, Haselnüsse, Orange, Zitrone und Äpfel in den Entsafter geben. Die Saftmischung in den Saftbehälter abfüllen und mit Honig, Zimt, Lebkuchengewürz und Kakaopulver vermengen.

» VIDEO
Wie mache ich Nussmilch?

NUTZEN

— gute Proteinquelle

 Küchengerät für beide Rezepte:

Bratapfel-Saft

Zutaten für 2 Gläser Saft

- *150 g Mandeln*
- *4 Äpfel*
- *1 Prise Zimt*
- *5 getrocknete und entsteinte Datteln*
- *1 Prise Vanillearoma*
- *½ Zitrone*
- *½ Glas Wasser*
- *50 g Rosinen*

Zubereitung

Die Mandeln und Datteln für mindestens 4 Stunden in Wasser einweichen. Danach das Wasser abgießen und die Mandeln spülen. Die Äpfel waschen, vierteln und bei Bedarf das Kerngehäuse entfernen. Die Äpfel mit Zimt bestreuen und mit Vanillearoma beträufeln. Von der Zitrone die Schale entfernen und die Frucht vierteln. Mandeln, Datteln, Äpfel, Zitrone und das halbe Glas Wasser in den Entsafter geben. Danach die Rosinen dazu.

TIPP

Zimt regt den Stoffwechsel an und senkt auf natürliche Weise den Blutzucker. Wer keine Rosinen mag, lässt sie einfach weg.

NUTZEN

— **regt den Stoffwechsel an**
— **wärmende Wirkung**
— **gute Proteinquelle**

Küchengerät: 

Pink Power

Zutaten für 2 Gläser Saft

› *150 g Mandeln*
› *5 getrocknete und entsteinte Datteln*
› *250 g Himbeeren*
› *¼ Ringelbete oder Rote Bete*
› *½ Limette*
› *1 Prise Vanillearoma*
› *1 Glas Wasser oder Kokoswasser*

Zubereitung

Die Mandeln und Datteln für mindestens 4 Stunden in Wasser einweichen. Danach das Wasser abgießen und die Mandeln spülen. Die Himbeeren und die Bete waschen. Von der Limette die Schale entfernen und die Frucht vierteln. Danach alles in den Entsafter geben.

NUTZEN

— gute Proteinquelle
— nährend und sättigend

Küchengerät: 

Rosa Milch

Zutaten für 2 Gläser Saft

- *150 g Cashewkerne*
- *1 Banane*
- *250 g gemischte Beeren*
- *1 Glas Wasser oder Kokoswasser*

Zubereitung

Die Cashewkerne für mindestens 4 Stunden in Wasser einweichen. Danach das Wasser abgießen und die Cashewkerne spülen. Die Banane schälen und die Beeren waschen. Alles in den Entsafter geben.

NUTZEN

— gute Proteinquelle
— nährend und sättigend
— Beauty-Elixier
— Anti-Aging

Tropical Coconut

Zutaten für 2 Gläser Saft

- *200 g Mandeln*
- *1 Mango*
- *150 g Erdbeeren*
- *½ Glas frisches Kokoswasser oder Kokosmilch*
- *¼ Ananas*

Zubereitung

Die Mandeln für mindestens 4 Stunden in Wasser einweichen. Danach das Wasser abgießen und die Mandeln spülen. Die Mango schälen und entkernen. Die Erdbeeren waschen. Von der Ananas die Schale entfernen und in Stücke schneiden. Alle Zutaten in den Entsafter geben.

NUTZEN

— sehr nährend und sättigend
— gute Proteinquelle
— Beauty-Elixier

Küchengerät für beide Rezepte: 

ROSA MILCH

TROPICAL COCONUT

Lavendel-Limo

SÄFTE

Zutaten für 2 Gläser Saft

- *1 Zitrone*
- *500 ml Kokoswasser*
- *1 Stängel Lavendel*

Zubereitung

Von der Zitrone die Schale entfernen und die Frucht vierteln. Lavendel waschen. Zitrone mit Kokoswasser und Lavendel in den Entsafter geben. Mit Eiswürfeln servieren.

TIPP

Bei Bedarf kann man noch etwas Honig in die Limo einrühren.

NUTZEN

— zur Erfrischung

 Küchengerät:

Kirsche-Birne

Zutaten für 2 Gläser Saft

- *4 Birnen*
- *400 g Kirschen*

Zubereitung

Birnen und Kirschen waschen. Bei Bedarf das Gehäuse der Birnen entfernen. Die Kirschen entkernen. Alle Zutaten in den Entsafter geben.

TIPP

Um die Fruchtsüße abzumildern, kann eine Zitrone oder Limette mitgepresst werden.

NUTZEN

— enthält viele Mineralstoffe und Spurenelemente
— ideal zum Abnehmen und Fasten

Küchengerät: 

Smoothies

After-Eight-Smoothie

Zutaten für 2 Gläser Smoothie

- *2 Bananen*
- *1 Stängel Minze*
- *2 TL Kakao*
- *2 kleine Gläser Kokosmilch*

Zubereitung

Die Bananen schälen, die Minze waschen. Den Kakao in die Kokosmilch geben und gut verrühren. Anschließend alle Zutaten in den Entsafter leeren und so lange im Saftbehälter vermischen, bis ein homogener Smoothie entstanden ist.

TIPP

Für eine dickere Konsistenz kann der Trester in den Smoothie eingerührt werden.

NUTZEN

— erfrischend

Das Rezept kann in allen diesen Küchengeräten zubereitet werden. Smoothies aus dem Entsafter werden schonender verarbeitet!

Tropisch Grün

Zutaten für 2 Gläser Smoothie

- *¼ Ananas*
- *1 Orange*
- *1 Stängel Minze*
- *2 Blätter Grünkohl*
- *1 Maracuja*
- *1 Glas Kokoswasser*

Zubereitung

Von der Ananas die Schale entfernen und in grobe Stücke schneiden. Die Orange schälen und die Frucht vierteln. Minze und Grünkohl waschen und in 5 cm lange Portionen schneiden. Maracuja aufschneiden und mit dem Löffel das Fruchtfleisch herausholen. Maracuja, Ananas, Orange, Minze und Grünkohl mit dem Kokoswasser in den Entsafter geben.

VARIATION

Der Grünkohl kann durch Spinat oder Sellerie ersetzt werden, die Ananas durch 1 Mango.

NUTZEN

— Stärkung des Immunsystems
— Vitaminbombe
— Energiekick
— Förderung der Verdauung
— ideal zum Abnehmen und Fasten

Das Rezept kann in allen diesen Küchengeräten zubereitet werden. Smoothies aus dem Entsafter werden schonender verarbeitet!

DETOX-SMOOTHIE

PROTEIN-BOMBE

Detox-Smoothie

Zutaten für 2 Gläser Smoothie

› *1 grüner Apfel*
› *2 Blätter Grünkohl*
(alternativ: 2 Stangen Sellerie)
› *½ Gurke*
› *4 cm Ingwer*
› *6 Blätter Löwenzahn*
› *3 Stängel Brennnessel*
› *1 kleines Glas Kokoswasser*

Zubereitung

Den Apfel schälen, vierteln und bei Bedarf das Kerngehäuse entfernen. Grünkohl, Gurke, Ingwer, Löwenzahn und Brennnesseln waschen. Grünkohl in 5 cm lange Portionen und Gurke in grobe Stücke schneiden. Alle Zutaten mit dem Kokoswasser in den Entsafter geben.

TIPP

Dieser Smoothie eignet sich ideal für eine Detoxkur im Frühjahr.

NUTZEN

— ideal zum Abnehmen und Fasten
— basische Wirkung
— regt den Stoffwechsel an
— für Diabetiker geeignet

Protein-Bombe

Zutaten für 2 Gläser Smoothie

› *200 g Mandeln*
› *100 g Spinat*
› *2 Bananen*
› *2 TL Chiasamen*
› *1 Glas Kokoswasser*

Zubereitung

Die Mandeln für mindestens 4 Stunden in Wasser einweichen. Danach das Wasser abgießen und die Mandeln spülen. Den Spinat waschen. Die Bananen schälen. Alle Zutaten – bis auf die Chiasamen – in den Entsafter geben. Nach dem Entsaften die Chiasamen in den Smoothie einrühren.

NUTZEN

— sehr nährend und sättigend
— gute Proteinquelle für Vegetarier und Veganer

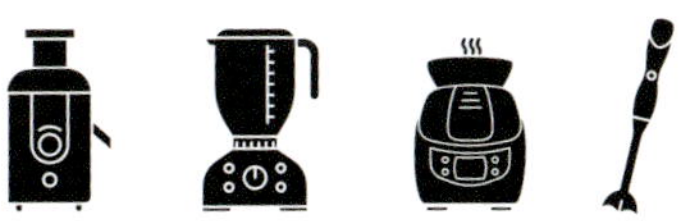

Die Rezepte können in allen diesen Küchengeräten zubereitet werden. Smoothies aus dem Entsafter werden schonender verarbeitet!

SMOOTHIES

Anti-Aging-Smoothie

Zutaten für 2 Gläser Smoothie

- *150 g Himbeeren*
- *150 g Blaubeeren*
- *½ Granatapfel oder 200 g Kirschen*
- *1 kleines Glas Kokoswasser*
- *2 TL Hanfsamen*

Zubereitung

Die Himbeeren und Blaubeeren waschen. Aus dem Granatapfel die Kerne herauslösen. Alle Zutaten – bis auf die Hanfsamen – in den Entsafter geben. Den Smoothie in Gläser füllen und die Hanfsamen darüberstreuen.

» VIDEO
Beeren im Fokus – Anti-Aging-Smoothie

VARIATION

Anstelle von Himbeeren und Blaubeeren können auch Erdbeeren oder Brombeeren verwendet werden.

NUTZEN

— Anti-Aging
— Beauty-Drink
— Vitaminbombe
— Stärkung des Immunsystems

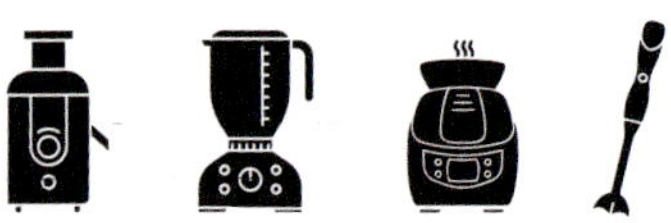

Das Rezept kann in allen diesen Küchengeräten zubereitet werden. Smoothies aus dem Entsafter werden schonender verarbeitet!

Für immer jung

Zutaten für 2 Gläser Smoothie

- *¼ Ananas*
- *200 g Trauben*
- *1 Orange*
- *4 cm frische Kurkuma*
- *2 TL Hanfsamen (alternativ Chiasamen)*
- *2 TL Leinsamen*
- *1 kleines Glas Kokoswasser*

Zubereitung

Von der Ananas die Schale entfernen und die Frucht in grobe Stücke schneiden. Trauben waschen und in kleine Portionen teilen. Von der Orange die Schale entfernen und das Fruchtfleisch vierteln. Die Kurkuma waschen, Ananas, Trauben, Orangen und Kurkuma mit dem Kokoswasser in den Entsafter geben. Danach den Hanf- und Leinsamen in den Smoothie rühren.

NUTZEN

— Anti-Aging
— Stärkung des Immunsystems
— Beauty-Elixier

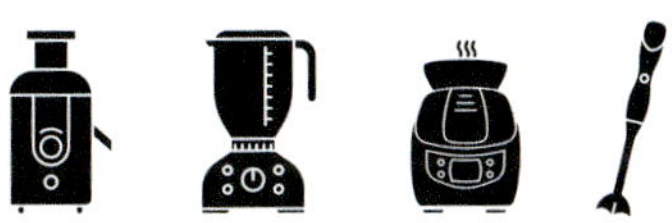

Das Rezept kann in allen diesen Küchengeräten zubereitet werden. Smoothies aus dem Entsafter werden schonender verarbeitet!

Stoffwechsel-Pusher

Zutaten für 2 Gläser Smoothie

- *2 Äpfel*
- *1 kleine Papaya*
- *¼ Ananas*
- *1 Zitrone*
- *1 Stängel Petersilie*
- *3 cm Ingwer*
- *4 cm Kurkuma*
- *1 Prise Cayenne-Pfeffer*

Zubereitung

Die Äpfel waschen, vierteln und bei Bedarf das Kerngehäuse entfernen. Die Äpfelviertel mit Cayenne-Pfeffer bestreuen. Die Papaya schälen und die Kerne entfernen. Die Ananas schälen und die Frucht in Stücke schneiden. Die Zitrone schälen und vierteln. Petersilie, Ingwer und Kurkuma waschen. Alle Zutaten in den Entsafter geben.

TIPP

Man kann auch ein paar Kerne der Papaya mitpressen. Sie geben ein zusätzlich scharfes Aroma. Die Kerne können auch getrocknet und als milder Pfeffer verwendet werden.

VARIATION

Diabetiker sollten süßes Obst wie Ananas weglassen und durch Grünes wie Spinat, Mangold oder Grünkohl ersetzen. Bei den Äpfeln grüne Sorten verwenden sowie Papayas, die noch leicht grünlich aussehen.

NUTZEN

— regt den Stoffwechsel an
— Energiekick
— Erfrischung
— zur Entgiftung
— Stärkung des Immunsystems
— Vitaminbombe
— Anti-Aging
— ideal zum Abnehmen und Fasten

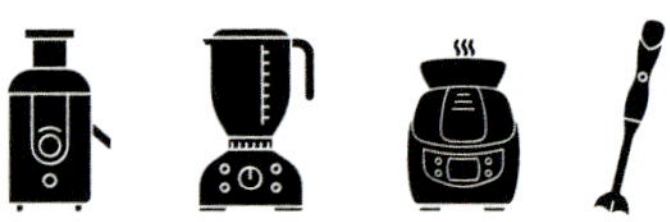

Das Rezept kann in allen diesen Küchengeräten zubereitet werden. Smoothies aus dem Entsafter werden schonender verarbeitet!

Entzündungs-Hemmer

Zutaten für 2 Gläser Smoothie

- *⅓ Ananas*
- *1 Mango*
- *2 Blätter Grünkohl*
- *1 Zitrone*
- *1 Glas Kokoswasser oder Saft einer frischen Kokosnuss*
- *3 cm frisches Kurkuma*
- *3 cm Ingwer*
- *2 Stängel Kräuter (wahlweise Petersilie, Minze, Wildkräuter)*
- *1 Prise Cayenne-Pfeffer*

Zubereitung

Von der Ananas die Schale entfernen und die Frucht in grobe Stücke schneiden. Auch die Mango schälen und entkernen. Den Grünkohl waschen und in 5 cm lange Stücke schneiden. Von der Zitrone die Schale entfernen und die Frucht vierteln. Die Kokosnuss öffnen und den Saft abfüllen. Kurkuma, Ingwer und Kräuter waschen. Den Cayenne-Pfeffer auf die Ananas streuen. Alle Zutaten in den Entsafter geben.

TIPP

Am besten schmeckt Kokoswasser, das direkt aus der Kokosnuss gewonnen wird.

VARIATION

Anstelle der Ananas und Mango können auch 2 Orangen gepresst werden.

NUTZEN

- Stärkung des Immunsystems
- Vitaminbombe
- Energiekick
- Förderung der Verdauung
- ideal zum Abnehmen und Fasten
- regt den Stoffwechsel an

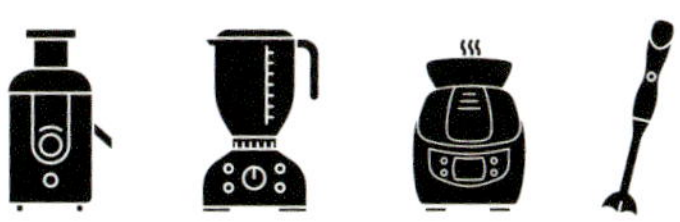

Das Rezept kann in allen diesen Küchengeräten zubereitet werden. Smoothies aus dem Entsafter werden schonender verarbeitet!

Brain-Power

Zutaten für 2 Gläser Smoothie

- *3 Bananen*
- *1 Glas Kokoswasser*
- *100 g Mandeln*
- *100 g Walnüsse*
- *2 TL Hanfsamen*
- *2 TL Leinsamen*

Zubereitung

Die Mandeln und Walnüsse für ca. 4 Stunden in Wasser einweichen. Danach Mandeln und Nüsse abspülen. Die Bananen schälen und halbieren. Mandeln, Nüsse, Bananen und Kokoswasser in den Entsafter geben. Danach Hanfsamen und Leinsamen in den fertigen Smoothie rühren.

TIPP

Anstelle der 3 Bananen kann man auch 3 Avocados verwenden. Avocados beinhalten wertvolle Omega-3-Fettsäuren.

NUTZEN

— Gehirnnahrung
— Beauty-Elixier
— Anti-Aging

Happy Vita

Zutaten für 2 Gläser Smoothie

- *200 g Brombeeren*
- *2 Pfirsiche*
- *1 Mango*
- *1 Maracuja*
- *1 Glas Kokoswasser*

Zubereitung

Brombeeren und Pfirsiche waschen. Pfirsiche entkernen. Mango schälen und entkernen. Maracuja halbieren und das Fruchtfleisch mit dem Löffel herauslösen. Alle Zutaten in den Entsafter geben.

NUTZEN

— Stärkung des Immunsystems
— Vitaminbombe
— Energiekick
— Anti-Aging
— Beauty-Elixier
— zur Erfrischung

Die Rezepte können in allen diesen Küchengeräten zubereitet werden. Smoothies aus dem Entsafter werden schonender verarbeitet!

BRAIN-POWER

HAPPY VITA

Green Energy

Zutaten für 2 Gläser Smoothie

- *⅓ Gurke*
- *¼ Ananas*
- *1 Banane*
- *½ Glas Kokosmilch*
- *1 Stängel Minze*
- *1 Handvoll Wildkräuter oder Spinat*

Zubereitung

Die Gurke waschen und in grobe Stücke schneiden. Von der Ananas und der Banane die Schale entfernen. Ananas und Banane in grobe Stücke schneiden. Minze und Wildkräuter waschen. Alle Zutaten in den Entsafter geben.

TIPP

Die Ananas hat ziemlich viele und harte Fasern. Daher sollte man diese Frucht immer am Schluss entsaften, damit die Fasern nicht zur Verstopfung des Entsafters führen.

NUTZEN

— Vitaminbombe
— Energiekick
— Förderung der Verdauung
— Muntermacher
— Beauty-Elixier
— zur Erfrischung
— regt den Stoffwechsel an

Das Rezept kann in allen diesen Küchengeräten zubereitet werden. Smoothies aus dem Entsafter werden schonender verarbeitet!

Wild und süß

Zutaten für 2 Gläser Smoothie

- *3 Äpfel*
- *300 g Trauben*
- *1 Handvoll Wildkräuter*

Zubereitung

Die Äpfel, Trauben und Wildkräuter waschen. Bei Bedarf das Kerngehäuse der Äpfel entfernen und die Äpfel vierteln. Trauben in kleinere Portionen teilen. Der Stiel muss nicht entfernt werden. Nacheinander alle Zutaten in den Entsafter geben.

NUTZEN

- Stärkung des Immunsystems
- Vitaminbombe
- Energiekick
- Förderung der Verdauung
- ideal zum Abnehmen und Fasten
- regt den Stoffwechsel an

TIPP

Je frischer die verwendeten Zutaten sind, desto mehr Nährstoffe sind darin enthalten. Ideal sind regional erzeugte Waren sowie Obst und Gemüse, das gerade Saison hat.

VARIATION

Diabetiker verwenden grüne Äpfel und anstelle der Trauben 500 g Grünes wie zum Beispiel eine Mischung aus Gurken, Spinat, Grünkohl, Mangold oder Feldsalat.

Das Rezept kann in allen diesen Küchengeräten zubereitet werden. Smoothies aus dem Entsafter werden schonender verarbeitet!

SOMMERFRISCHE

BUNTER OBSTMIX

Sommerfrische

Zutaten für 2 Gläser Smoothie

› *½ Galia-Melone*
› *¼ Melone*
› *200 g Erdbeeren*

Zubereitung

Aus den Melonen das Fruchtfleisch herauslösen und in grobe Stücke schneiden. Die Erdbeeren waschen. Alle Zutaten in den Entsafter geben.

TIPP

Um die Fruchtsüße abzumildern, kann eine Zitrone oder Limette mitgepresst werden.

NUTZEN

— Vitaminbombe
— Energiekick
— ideal nach dem Sport
— Muntermacher

Bunter Obstmix

Zutaten für 2 Gläser Smoothie

› *¼ Ananas*
› *1 Apfel*
› *1 Pfirsich*
› *1 Granatapfel*
› *1 Orange*

Zubereitung

Von der Ananas die Schale entfernen und die Frucht in grobe Stücke schneiden. Den Apfel waschen, bei Bedarf das Kerngehäuse entfernen und den Apfel vierteln. Den Pfirsich waschen, entkernen und vierteln. Die Kerne aus dem Granatapfel lösen. Von der Orange die Schale entfernen und die Frucht in Viertel schneiden. Alle Zutaten in den Entsafter geben.

NUTZEN

— Stärkung des Immunsystems
— Vitaminbombe
— Energiekick
— Förderung der Verdauung
— Anti-Aging
— Beauty-Elixier

Die Rezepte können in allen diesen Küchengeräten zubereitet werden. Smoothies aus dem Entsafter werden schonender verarbeitet!

Suppen

Mango-Chili-Süßkartoffelsuppe

Zutaten für 2 Portionen Suppe

- *2 Mangos*
- *2 Süßkartoffeln*
- *1 Glas Kokosmilch*
- *1 Zitrone*
- *3 cm Kurkuma*
- *1 Prise Chili*
- *1 Prise Salz*
- *1 Prise Pfeffer*
- *1 Prise Curry*

Zubereitung

Von den Mangos und den Süßkartoffeln die Schale entfernen. Die Mangos entkernen und in Stücke schneiden. Süßkartoffeln ebenfalls in Stücke schneiden. Von der Zitrone die Schale entfernen und die Frucht vierteln. Kurkuma waschen. Zum Entsaften das grobe Sieb verwenden. Mangos, Kurkuma, Süßkartoffeln und Zitrone mit der Kokosmilch in den Entsafter geben. Die Suppe in den Saftbehälter abfüllen und mit Chili, Salz, Curry und Pfeffer würzen.

TIPP

Die Suppe kann leicht erhitzt oder im Dörrgerät erwärmt werden. Wenn die Suppe einige Stunden im Dörrgerät getrocknet wird, intensiviert sich der Geschmack. Zu dieser Suppe passen auch frische Kräuter wie Minze, Petersilie, Basilikum oder Koriander.

NUTZEN

— Stärkung des Immunsystems
— Vitaminbombe
— Energiekick
— wärmende Wirkung

Das Rezept kann in allen diesen Küchengeräten zubereitet werden. Suppen aus dem Entsafter werden schonender verarbeitet!

Möhrensuppe

SUPPEN

Zutaten für 2 Portionen Suppe

- *150 g Cashewkerne*
- *5 Möhren*
- *1 Frühlingszwiebel*
- *2 cm Kurkuma*
- *½ Orange*
- *½ Glas Kokosmilch*
- *1 Prise Salz*
- *1 Prise Pfeffer*
- *1 Prise Chili*
- *2 EL Olivenöl*
- *1 TL Gemüsebrühe-Pulver (optional)*

Zum Garnieren

- *Basilikum*
- *2 TL Schmand*
- *Kürbis- und Sonnenblumenkerne*

Zubereitung

Cashewkerne für ca. 4 Stunden in Wasser einweichen und abspülen. Möhren, Frühlingszwiebel und Kurkuma waschen. Möhren und Frühlingszwiebel in grobe Streifen schneiden. Von der Orange die Schale entfernen und die Frucht vierteln. Möhren, Frühlingszwiebel, Orange, Cashewkerne und Kurkuma zusammen mit der Kokosmilch in den Entsafter geben. Dazu das grobe Sieb verwenden. Die Suppe in den Saftbehälter abfüllen und mit Salz, Pfeffer, Chili, Olivenöl und Gemüsebrühe würzen. Anschließend mit Kürbiskernen, Sonnenblumenkernen, Basilikum und Schmand garnieren.

NUTZEN

— Stärkung des Immunsystems
— Vitaminbombe
— Energiekick
— nährend und sättigend

Das Rezept kann in allen diesen Küchengeräten zubereitet werden. Suppen aus dem Entsafter werden schonender verarbeitet!

Curry-Kokos-Suppe

Zutaten für 2 Portionen Suppe

- *200 g Cashewkerne*
- *2 Möhren*
- *2 cm Ingwer*
- *2 cm Kurkuma*
- *1 Mango*
- *1 Limette*
- *1 Glas Kokosmilch*
- *1 EL Curry*
- *1 Prise Salz*
- *1 Prise Pfeffer*
- *1 Prise Chili*
- *2–3 Stängel frische Kräuter (Petersilie oder Koriander)*
- *1 TL Gemüsebrühe-Pulver (optional)*

Zum Garnieren

- *frischer Chili*
- *Kürbiskerne*
- *Kokosflocken*

Zubereitung

Cashewkerne für mindestens 4 Stunden in Wasser einweichen und anschließend das Wasser abgießen. Möhren, Ingwer und Kurkuma waschen. Von der Mango die Schale und den Kern entfernen, die Frucht vierteln. Von der Limette die Schale entfernen und die Frucht vierteln. Die Cashewkerne mit den Möhren, der Mango, der Limette, Kurkuma, Ingwer, den Kräutern und der Kokosmilch in den Entsafter geben. In den Saftbehälter abfüllen und mit Curry, Salz, Pfeffer, Chili und Gemüsebrühe würzen. Anschließend die Suppe mit Chili, Kürbiskernen und Kokosflocken garnieren.

NUTZEN

— gute Proteinquelle

— wärmende Wirkung

Das Rezept kann in allen diesen Küchengeräten zubereitet werden. Suppen aus dem Entsafter werden schonender verarbeitet!

Gazpacho

Zutaten für 2 Portionen Suppe

- *100 g Cashewkerne*
- *300 g Cocktailtomaten*
- *1 rote Paprika*
- *1 Minigurke*
- *1 Frühlingszwiebel*
- *1 Stängel Basilikum*
- *1 Knoblauchzehe*
- *½ Zitrone*
- *1 Prise Salz*
- *1 Prise Pfeffer*
- *1 Prise Chili*
- *2 EL Olivenöl*
- *1 TL Gemüsebrühe-Pulver (optional)*

zum Garnieren

- *Basilikumblätter*
- *3–4 getrocknete und in Olivenöl eingelegte Tomaten*
- *geriebener Parmesan*

Zubereitung

Die Cashewkerne für ca. 4 Stunden in Wasser einweichen. Danach Wasser abgießen und Cashews spülen. Cocktailtomaten, Paprika, Minigurke, Frühlingszwiebel und Basilikum waschen. Cocktailtomaten bei Bedarf halbieren, Paprika, Gurke und Frühlingszwiebel in Streifen schneiden. Knoblauchzehe schälen. Von der Zitrone die Schale entfernen und die Frucht vierteln. Anschließend die Tomaten, Paprika, Gurke, Frühlingszwiebel, Zitrone, Knoblauch und die eingeweichten Cashewkerne in den Entsafter geben. Dazu das grobe Sieb verwenden. Die Suppe in den Saftbehälter abfüllen und mit Salz, Pfeffer, Chili, Olivenöl und Gemüsebrühe würzen. Mit dem Basilikum, dem Parmesan und den klein geschnittenen Tomaten garnieren.

NUTZEN

— Stärkung des Immunsystems
— Vitaminbombe
— Energiekick
— Anti-Aging

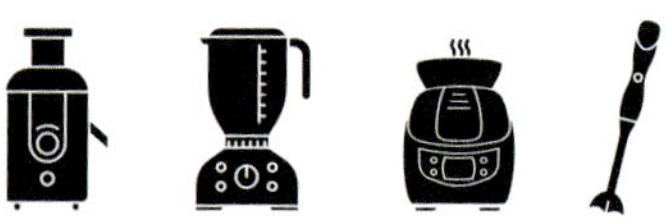

Das Rezept kann in allen diesen Küchengeräten zubereitet werden. Suppen aus dem Entsafter werden schonender verarbeitet!

SUPPEN

Avocado-Suppe

Zutaten für 2 Portionen Suppe

- *2 kleine Zucchini*
- *1 Frühlingszwiebel*
- *2 Stängel Petersilie*
- *2 Avocados*
- *1 Limette*
- *1 Prise Salz*
- *1 Prise Pfeffer*
- *1 TL Honig*
- *1 EL Olivenöl*
- *1 TL Gemüsebrühe-Pulver (optional)*

Zubereitung

Die Zucchini, Frühlingszwiebel und Petersilie waschen. Zucchini und Frühlingszwiebel in Stücke schneiden. Von den Avocados die Schale und den Kern entfernen. Von der Limette ebenfalls die Schale entfernen und die Frucht vierteln. Avocados, Zucchini, Frühlingszwiebel und Zitrone in den Entsafter geben. Die Suppe in den Saftbehälter abfüllen und mit Salz, Pfeffer, Honig, Olivenöl und Gemüsebrühe würzen. Zum Schluss gehackte Petersilie über die Suppe streuen.

NUTZEN

- Anti-Aging
- Beauty-Elixier
- Gehirnnahrung

Das Rezept kann in allen diesen Küchengeräten zubereitet werden. Suppen aus dem Entsafter werden schonender verarbeitet!

Guacamole-Suppe

Zutaten für 2 Portionen Suppe

- *3 Avocados*
- *1 Limette*
- *4 Cocktailtomaten*
- *2 Stängel Petersilie*
- *1 rote Zwiebel*
- *1 Prise Salz*
- *1 Prise Pfeffer*
- *1 Prise Chili*

Zubereitung

Von den Avocados die Schale entfernen und Kerne herauslösen. Die Limette schälen und vierteln. Avocados und Limette in den Entsafter geben. Die fertige Guacamole-Suppe in ein Gefäß leeren. Tomaten und Petersilie waschen, von der Zwiebel die Schale entfernen. Die Tomaten und Zwiebel fein würfeln, die Petersilie fein hacken. Die Tomaten, Zwiebel und Petersilie unter die Guacamole-Suppe rühren und mit Salz, Pfeffer und Chili abschmecken.

NUTZEN

— Anti-Aging

— Beauty-Elixier

Das Rezept kann in allen diesen Küchengeräten zubereitet werden. Suppen aus dem Entsafter werden schonender verarbeitet!

Brokkoli-Blumenkohlsuppe

Zutaten für 2 Portionen Suppe

- *300 g Blumenkohl*
- *300 g Brokkoli*
- *1 EL Apfelessig*
- *1 EL Honig*
- *1 Prise Salz*
- *1 Prise Pfeffer*
- *1 Prise Muskat*
- *1 TL Gemüsebrühe-Pulver (optional)*
- *2 EL Crème fraîche*

Zum Garnieren

- *geröstete Mandeln, Petersilie und geröstete Zwiebeln*

Zubereitung

Blumenkohl und Brokkoli waschen und in kleine Portionen schneiden. Alles in den Entsafter geben. Dafür das grobe Sieb verwenden. Gemisch in einem Topf kurz köcheln lassen und dann mit Apfelessig, Honig, Salz, Pfeffer, Muskat, Gemüsebrühe und Crème fraîche verrühren. 1 Zwiebel klein schneiden und in 1 EL Kokosöl anrösten. Eventuell 1 Esslöffel Mandelblättchen dazugeben. Petersilie fein hacken und zur Suppe geben. Mit gerösteten Zwiebeln und Mandeln verzieren.

NUTZEN

— Stärkung des Immunsystems
— Vitaminbombe
— Energiekick

Das Rezept kann in allen diesen Küchengeräten zubereitet werden. Suppen aus dem Entsafter werden schonender verarbeitet!

Erntesuppe

Zutaten für 2 Portionen Suppe

- *2 kleine Paprika, rot und gelb*
- *1 Zucchini*
- *200 g Cocktailtomaten*
- *2 Möhren*
- *1 Frühlingszwiebel*
- *2 cm Ingwer*
- *2 cm Kurkuma*
- *1 Prise Salz*
- *1 Prise Pfeffer*
- *1 Prise Chili*
- *1 kleiner Stängel Rosmarin*
- *1 Stängel Basilikum*
- *2 EL Olivenöl*
- *1 TL Gemüsebrühe-Pulver (optional)*
- *1 Handvoll frische Kresse*
- *2 Stängel Petersilie*

Zubereitung

Paprika, Zucchini, Tomaten, Möhren, Frühlingszwiebel, Ingwer, Kurkuma, Rosmarin, Basilikum, Petersilie und Kresse waschen. Paprika, Zucchini, Möhren und Frühlingszwiebel in grobe Streifen schneiden. Tomaten halbieren. Paprika, Zucchini, Möhren, Frühlingszwiebel, Tomaten, Kurkuma, Ingwer, Rosmarin und Basilikum in den Entsafter geben. Die Suppe in den Saftbehälter abfüllen und mit Salz, Pfeffer, Chili, Gemüsebrühe und Olivenöl würzen. Die Petersilie fein hacken. Mit der frischen Kresse und gehackten Petersilie garnieren.

TIPP

Für Suppen immer das grobe Sieb des Entsafters verwenden. Wer die Suppe sämiger mag, gibt einfach den Trester in das Suppen-Gemisch zurück.

NUTZEN

— Stärkung des Immunsystems
— Vitaminbombe
— Energiekick
— schneller Elektrolyt-Ausgleich

Das Rezept kann in allen diesen Küchengeräten zubereitet werden. Suppen aus dem Entsafter werden schonender verarbeitet!

Rote-Bete-Suppe

Zutaten für 2 Portionen Suppe

- *2–3 Rote Beten*
- *1 Apfel*
- *1 Orange*
- *4 cm Ingwer oder frischer Meerrettich*
- *1 Frühlingszwiebel*
- *1 Prise Salz*
- *1 Prise Pfeffer*
- *1 TL Gemüsebrühe-Pulver (optional)*
- *1 TL Kokosflocken*
- *etwas Dill zum Garnieren*

Zubereitung

Die Rote Bete und den Apfel waschen und vierteln. Bei Bedarf das Kerngehäuse aus dem Apfel schneiden. Die Rote Bete vierteln. Von der Orange die Schale dünn abschneiden. Ingwer und Frühlingszwiebel waschen. Frühlingszwiebel in Stücke schneiden. Alle Zutaten in den Entsafter geben. Die Suppe in den Saftbehälter abfüllen und mit Salz, Pfeffer und Gemüsebrühe würzen. Die Suppe mit Kokosflocken und Dill garnieren.

TIPP

Wer die Suppe noch cremiger mag, kann 2 EL Crème fraîche einrühren.

NUTZEN

— Stärkung des Immunsystems
— Vitaminbombe
— Energiekick

Das Rezept kann in allen diesen Küchengeräten zubereitet werden. Suppen aus dem Entsafter werden schonender verarbeitet!

Aprikosen-Tomaten-Suppe

Zutaten für 2 Portionen Suppe

- *8 Aprikosen*
- *2 gelbe Minipaprika*
- *10 gelbe Cocktailtomaten*
- *2 cm Kurkuma*
- *1 Stängel Zitronenmelisse*
- *1 Stängel Minze*
- *1 Prise Chili*
- *1 Prise Salz*
- *1 Prise Pfeffer*

Zubereitung

Aprikosen, Paprika, Tomaten, Kurkuma, Zitronenmelisse und Minze waschen. Aprikosen entkernen und vierteln, Paprika in Streifen schneiden, Tomaten halbieren. Aprikosen, Paprika, Tomaten, Kurkuma, Zitronenmelisse und Minze in den Entsafter geben. In den Saftbehälter abfüllen und mit Chili, Salz und Pfeffer würzen.

NUTZEN

— Stärkung des Immunsystems
— Vitaminbombe
— Energiekick
— Anti-Aging
— Beauty-Elixier

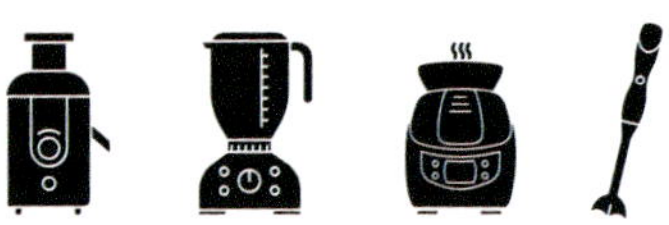

Das Rezept kann in allen diesen Küchengeräten zubereitet werden. Suppen aus dem Entsafter werden schonender verarbeitet!

Melonen-Gurken-Suppe

Zutaten für 2 Portionen Suppe

› *3 kleine Gartengurken*
› *¼ Wassermelone*
› *1 Stängel Minze*
› *1 EL Himbeeressig*
› *1 Prise Salz*
› *1 Prise Pfeffer*

Zubereitung

Die Gurken waschen und in Stücke schneiden. Minze ebenfalls waschen. Fruchtfleisch aus der Melone lösen und in kleine Stücke schneiden. Gurken, Melone und Minze in den Entsafter geben. In den Saftbehälter abfüllen und mit Himbeeressig, Pfeffer und Salz würzen.

NUTZEN

— ideal nach dem Sport
— schneller Elektrolyt-Ausgleich
— kühlende Wirkung

Das Rezept kann in allen diesen Küchengeräten zubereitet werden. Suppen aus dem Entsafter werden schonender verarbeitet!

Desserts

DESSERTS

Nuss-Mus

Zutaten für 1 Schale Nussmus

- *300 g Haselnüsse, Mandeln und Walnüsse, gemischt*
- *3 EL Kokosöl*
- *3 EL Honig*
- *1 Prise Salz*
- *1 Prise Vanille-Aroma*

Zubereitung

Die Nüsse und Mandeln ca. 4 Stunden in Wasser einweichen. Danach das Wasser abgießen und die Mandeln und Nüsse gut durchspülen. In den Entsafter geben und mit dem groben Sieb gut durchmischen. Das Pressgut mit dem Trester wieder vermischen. Anschließend die Masse in ein Gefäß geben und mit dem Kokosöl, Honig, Salz sowie Vanille-Aroma zu einer homogenen Masse vermengen.

Das Rezept kann in allen diesen Küchengeräten zubereitet werden. Desserts aus dem Entsafter werden schonender verarbeitet!

Pflaumen-Mus

Zutaten für 4 Portionen Mus

- *600 g Pflaumen*
- *600 g Brombeeren*
- *1 Prise Vanille-Aroma*
- *1 Prise Zimt*
- *2 EL Amaretto (optional)*
- *500 g Gelierzucker*

Zubereitung

Die Pflaumen und Brombeeren waschen. Die Pflaumen entsteinen und mit den Brombeeren in den Entsafter geben. Das entstandene Gemisch in einen großen Topf geben. Vanille-Aroma, Zimt und Amaretto hinzufügen. Gelierzucker dazugeben, gut durchmischen und 4 Minuten kochen. Anschließend in mit heißem Wasser ausgespülte Gläser abfüllen.

Apfel-Zimt-Mus

Zutaten für 4 Gläser Mus

- *1,2 kg Äpfel*
- *1 Prise Zimt*
- *Vanille-Aroma*
- *1 Zitrone*

Zubereitung

Die Äpfel waschen. Bei Bedarf das Kerngehäuse entfernen und die Äpfel vierteln. Die Viertel mit Zimt bestreuen und mit Vanillearoma beträufeln. Von der Zitrone die Schale entfernen und die Frucht ebenfalls vierteln. Äpfel und Zitrone in den Entsafter geben. Hierfür das grobe Sieb verwenden.

TIPP

Ideal für ältere oder kranke Menschen, die nicht so gut kauen können.

NUTZEN

— Stärkung des Immunsystems
— Vitaminbombe
— Energiekick
— Förderung der Verdauung
— wärmende Wirkung

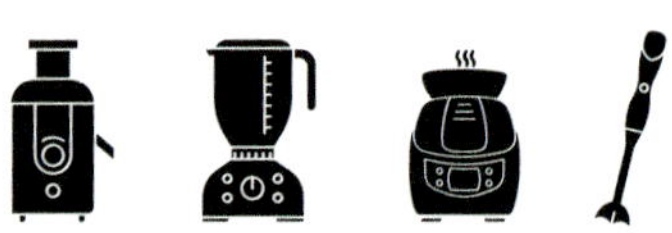

Die Rezepte können in allen diesen Küchengeräten zubereitet werden. Desserts aus dem Entsafter werden schonender verarbeitet!

PFLAUMEN-MUS

APFEL-ZIMT-MUS

» VIDEO
Eiscreme und Sorbet aus dem Entsafter

Erdbeer-Himbeer-Sorbet

Zutaten für 4 Portionen Sorbet

- *500 g Erdbeeren*
- *500 g Himbeeren*
- *1 Zitrone*
- *6 EL Honig*

Zubereitung

Die Erdbeeren und Himbeeren waschen. Von der Zitrone die Schale entfernen und die Frucht vierteln. Erdbeeren, Himbeeren und Zitrone in den Entsafter geben und danach in ein Gefäß abfüllen. Anschließend Honig dazugeben und gut verrühren. Das Gemisch in eine Form füllen und für einige Stunden in den Gefrierschrank stellen.

TIPP

Silikonförmchen eignen sich wunderbar für dieses selbst gemachte Sorbet.

NUTZEN

— Vitaminbombe
— Beauty-Elixier

Das Rezept kann in allen diesen Küchengeräten zubereitet werden. Desserts aus dem Entsafter werden schonender verarbeitet!

Mango-Kokos-Eis

Zutaten für 4 Portionen Eis

- *3 Mangos*
- *½ Limette*
- *200 ml Kokosmilch*
- *2 EL Honig*

Zubereitung

Von den Mangos die Schale und den Kern entfernen und die Früchte vierteln. Von der Limette ebenfalls die Schale entfernen und die Frucht vierteln. Mangos und Limette mit der Kokosmilch in den Entsafter geben. In ein Gefäß abfüllen, den Honig einrühren und alles gut vermischen. Die Masse in den Gefrierschrank geben und mehrere Stunden kalt stellen.

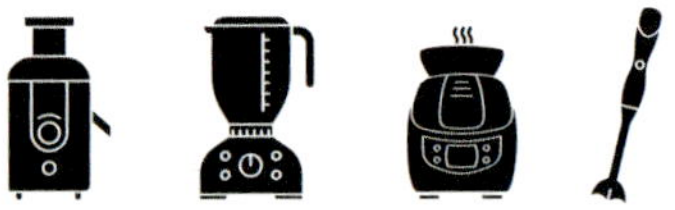

Das Rezept kann in allen diesen Küchengeräten zubereitet werden. Desserts aus dem Entsafter werden schonender verarbeitet!

Brombeer-Eis

Zutaten für 4 Portionen Eis

- *600 g Brombeeren*
- *6 EL Honig*

Zubereitung

Die Brombeeren waschen und in den Entsafter geben. In ein Gefäß abfüllen, den Honig in den Saft einrühren und gut vermischen. Anschließend in den Gefrierschrank geben und mehrere Stunden kalt stellen.

NUTZEN

— Vitaminbombe

Zitronen-Eiscreme

Zutaten für 4 Portionen Eiscreme

- *3 Zitronen*
- *500 ml Kokosmilch*
- *4 EL Honig*

Zubereitung

Von den Zitronen die Schale entfernen und die Zitronen vierteln. Zusammen mit der Kokosmilch in den Entsafter geben und in ein Gefäß abfüllen. Danach den Honig einrühren und alles gut vermischen. Die Masse in Formen füllen und im Gefrierschrank mehrere Stunden kalt stellen.

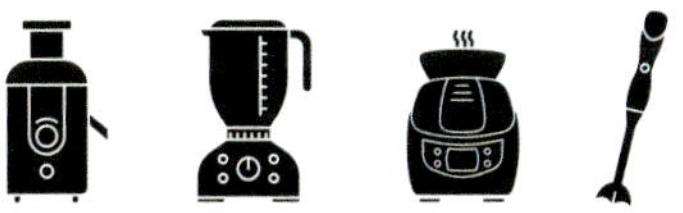

Die Rezepte können in allen diesen Küchengeräten zubereitet werden. Desserts aus dem Entsafter werden schonender verarbeitet!

Dreifarbiges Fruchteis

Zutaten für 4 Portionen Eis

- *200 g Brombeeren*
- *200 g Erdbeeren*
- *200 g Aprikosen*
- *¾ Zitrone*
- *3 EL Honig (optional)*

Zubereitung

Die Brombeeren, Erdbeeren und Aprikosen waschen. Aus den Aprikosen den Kern herauslösen. Von der Zitrone die Schale abschneiden und die Frucht vierteln. Zunächst die Brombeeren mit einem Viertel Zitrone entsaften. In ein Glas abfüllen. Anschließend die Erdbeeren mit einem Viertel Zitrone entsaften und in ein Glas abfüllen. Die Aprikosen ebenfalls mit einem Viertel Zitrone entsaften und in ein Glas abfüllen. Nun in jedes Glas einen Esslöffel Honig einrühren. Zuerst eine Schicht Brombeer-Mischung in eine Form geben und anfrosten lassen. Wenn die Masse angefroren ist, die Erdbeer-Mischung einfüllen und wieder anfrosten lassen. Zum Schluss die Aprikosen-Mischung in die Eisform füllen und alles gut durchfrieren lassen.

NUTZEN
— Vitaminbombe

Das Rezept kann in allen diesen Küchengeräten zubereitet werden. Desserts aus dem Entsafter werden schonender verarbeitet!

Gesunde Nusscreme

Zutaten für eine Schale Nusscreme

- *250 g Haselnüsse, Mandeln und Walnüsse gemischt*
- *3 EL Kokosöl*
- *3–4 EL Honig*
- *1 Prise Salz*
- *3 EL Kakaopulver*
- *1 Prise Vanille-Aroma*

Zubereitung

Die Nüsse und Mandeln ca. 4 Stunden in Wasser einweichen. Danach das Wasser abgießen. Die Mandeln und Nüsse in den Entsafter geben und mit dem groben Sieb entsaften. Das Pressgut mit dem Trester wieder vermischen. Die Mischung in ein Gefäß geben und mit dem Kokosöl, Honig, Salz, Kakaopulver und Vanille-Aroma zu einer homogenen Masse verrühren.

NUTZEN

— guter Lieferant für Proteine

Das Rezept kann in allen diesen Küchengeräten zubereitet werden. Desserts aus dem Entsafter werden schonender verarbeitet!

Breie...

Avocado-Brei

Zutaten für 1 Portion Brei

- *1 Avocado*
- *2 Babybananen*
- *½ Zucchini*
- *¼ Zitrone*

Zubereitung

Von der Avocado die Schale und den Kern entfernen und die Avocado vierteln. Die Babybananen schälen und halbieren. Die Zucchini waschen und in grobe Stücke schneiden. Von der Zitrone die Schale entfernen und vierteln. Alle Zutaten in den Entsafter geben.

NUTZEN

— Anti-Aging
— Beauty-Elixier
— Ideal für Menschen, die nicht mehr gut kauen können

Das Rezept kann in allen diesen Küchengeräten zubereitet werden. Breie aus dem Entsafter werden schonender verarbeitet!

Shots

Shots sind konzentrierte Säfte, die nur in kleinen Mengen (etwa ein kleines Glas oder Schnapsglas) konsumiert werden. Die Zutaten von Shots sind meist sehr intensiv und nährstoffreich, wie z. B. Kurkuma, Ingwer, Kräuter, Sprossen oder Weizengras, und gelten als Immunbooster.

GELBES FEUERWASSER

FEUER-SHOT

Gelbes Feuerwasser

Zutaten für 2 Gläser Shot

- *4 cm Kurkuma*
- *4 cm Ingwer*
- *1 Zitrone*
- *1 kleines Glas warmes Wasser*
- *1 EL Honig*
- *1 Prise Salz*
- *1 EL Apfelessig*
- *1 Prise Zimt*
- *1 Prise Pfeffer*

Zubereitung

Kurkuma und Ingwer waschen. Von der Zitrone die Schale entfernen und die Frucht vierteln. Kurkuma, Ingwer, Zitrone und das Wasser in den Entsafter geben. In den Saftbehälter abfüllen und mit Honig, Salz, Apfelessig, Zimt und Pfeffer verrühren.

NUTZEN

— Stärkung des Immunsystems
— Energiekick
— Förderung der Verdauung
— ideal zum Abnehmen und Fasten
— wärmende Wirkung
— Muntermacher
— regt den Stoffwechsel an

Feuer-Shot

Zutaten für 2 Gläser Shot

- *200 g Holunderbeeren*
- *3 cm Ingwer*
- *3 cm Kurkuma*
- *½ Zitrone*
- *1 halbes Glas Kokoswasser*
- *1 EL Honig*
- *1 Prise Salz*
- *1 Prise Pfeffer*

Zubereitung

Holunderbeeren, Ingwer und Kurkuma waschen. Von der Zitrone die Schale entfernen und die Frucht vierteln. Holunderbeeren, Ingwer, Kurkuma, Zitrone und das Kokoswasser in den Entsafter geben. In den Saftbehälter abfüllen und mit Honig, Salz und Pfeffer verrühren.

NUTZEN

— Stärkung des Immunsystems
— Energiekick
— Förderung der Verdauung
— ideal zum Abnehmen und Fasten
— wärmende Wirkung
— Muntermacher
— regt den Stoffwechsel an

Küchengerät für beide Rezepte: 

Kurkuma-Shot

Zutaten für 2 Gläser Shot

- *6 cm Kurkuma*
- *1 Orange*
- *½ Zitrone*
- *1 Prise Salz*
- *1 Prise Zimt*
- *1 Prise Pfeffer*
- *1 halbes Glas Kokoswasser*
- *2 TL Honig*

Zubereitung

Kurkuma waschen. Von der Orange und der Zitrone die Schale entfernen und die Früchte vierteln. Kurkuma, Orange, Zitrone und das Kokoswasser in den Entsafter geben. In den Saftbehälter abfüllen und mit Salz, Zimt, Pfeffer und Honig verrühren.

» VIDEO
Kurkuma-Shot mit Infos zu Vitalstoffen

NUTZEN

- Stärkung des Immunsystems
- Energiekick
- Förderung der Verdauung
- ideal zum Abnehmen und Fasten
- wärmende Wirkung
- Muntermacher
- regt den Stoffwechsel an

 Küchengerät: 

Weizengras-Shot

SHOTS

Zutaten für 2 Gläser Shot

- *200 g frisches Weizengras*
- *½ Zitrone*
- *⅓ Ananas*
- *1 Maracuja*

Zubereitung

Weizengras waschen und in Stücke schneiden. Von der Zitrone die Schale abschneiden und die Frucht vierteln. Die Ananas schälen und in grobe Stücke schneiden. Die Maracuja aufschneiden und das Fruchtfleisch mit dem Löffel herausholen. Alle Zutaten in den Entsafter geben.

NUTZEN

— Stärkung des Immunsystems
— Vitaminbombe
— Energiekick
— Förderung der Verdauung
— ideal zum Abnehmen und Fasten
— Anti-Aging
— regt den Stoffwechsel an

Küchengerät: 

Rote-Bete-Shot

Zutaten für 2 Gläser Shot

- *2 Rote Beten*
- *3 cm Ingwer*

Zubereitung

Rote Beten und Ingwer waschen und in Stücke schneiden. Beides in den Entsafter geben.

NUTZEN

— Stärkung des Immunsystems
— Energiekick
— Förderung der Verdauung
— ideal zum Abnehmen und Fasten
— basische Wirkung
— Anti-Aging
— wärmende Wirkung

Super-Green-Shot

Zutaten für 2 Gläser Shot

- *100 g Spinat*
- *2 Blätter Grünkohl*
- *½ Zitrone*
- *2 Stängel Minze*
- *1 EL Chlorella-Pulver*
- *1 EL Spirulina-Pulver*

Zubereitung

Spinat und Grünkohl waschen und in grobe Stücke schneiden. Von der Zitrone die Schale abschneiden und die Frucht vierteln. Die Minze waschen. Spinat, Grünkohl, Zitrone und Minze in den Entsafter geben. In den Saftbehälter abfüllen und Spirulina- sowie Chlorella-Pulver in den Saft rühren.

NUTZEN

— Stärkung des Immunsystems
— Vitaminbombe
— Energiekick
— Förderung der Verdauung
— ideal zum Abnehmen und Fasten
— basische Wirkung
— regt den Stoffwechsel an

 Küchengerät für beide Rezepte: 

ROTE-BETE-SHOT

SUPER-GREEN-SHOT

Sprossen-Shot

Zutaten für 2 Gläser Shot

- *100 g gemischte Sprossen*
- *⅓ Gurke*
- *1 Zitrone*

Zubereitung

Die Sprossen und die Gurke waschen. Gurke in Stücke schneiden. Von der Zitrone die Schale abschneiden und die Frucht vierteln. Alle Zutaten in den Entsafter geben.

NUTZEN

— Stärkung des Immunsystems
— Vitaminbombe
— Energiekick
— Förderung der Verdauung
— ideal zum Abnehmen und Fasten
— Anti-Aging
— regt den Stoffwechsel an

Küchengerät:

Haut-Elixier-Shot

Zutaten für 2 Gläser Shot

- *1 Blatt Aloe vera*
- *⅓ Gurke*
- *1 Orange, ½ Zitrone*
- *1 EL Honig*
- *1 EL Chiasamen*

Zubereitung

Aloe vera aufschneiden und das Filet herauslösen. Die Gurke waschen und in Stücke schneiden. Die Orange und Zitrone schälen und vierteln. Aloe vera, Gurke, Orange und Zitrone in den Entsafter geben. In den Saftbehälter abfüllen und Honig sowie Chiasamen einrühren.

NUTZEN

— Anti-Aging
— Beauty-Elixier

Parasiten-Killer-Shot

Zutaten für 2 Gläser Shot

- *1 kleiner Rettich oder 6 Radieschen*
- *3 cm Ingwer*
- *1 kleine Zwiebel*
- *½ Zitrone*
- *1 kleines Glas warmes Wasser*
- *1 EL Honig*

Zubereitung

Rettich und Ingwer waschen, Rettich in grobe Stücke schneiden. Zwiebel und Zitrone schälen und beides vierteln. Rettich, Zwiebel und Ingwer mit dem Wasser in den Entsafter geben. In den Saftbehälter abfüllen und Honig einrühren.

NUTZEN

— regt den Stoffwechsel an

Küchengerät für beide Rezepte: 

Über die Autorin

Diana Pyter arbeitet seit mehr als 25 Jahren als Journalistin und Autorin. Sie hat bereits 20 Bücher publiziert und beschäftigt sich seit vielen Jahren mit gesunder Ernährung und einer bewussten Lebensweise. Ihr Wissen und ihre positiven Erfahrungen mit frisch gepressten Säften, Smoothies, Suppen und Shots sowie vitalstoffreicher Ernährung im Allgemeinen gibt die studierte Germanistin und Kommunikationswissenschaftlerin über ihre Firma HAPPY VITA sowie im Rahmen von Vorträgen weiter. Sie lebt mit ihrem Mann und ihren zwei Kindern im bayerischen Augsburg.

www.happy-vita.de

Aprikosen-Bananen-Brei

Zutaten für 1 Portion Brei

- *5 reife Aprikosen*
- *2 Babybananen*

Zubereitung

Die Aprikosen waschen, entkernen und vierteln. Die Bananen schälen. Aprikosen und Bananen in den Entsafter geben.

TIPP

Je nach Geschmack könnte man auch noch ein paar Cashewkerne dazugeben. Das macht den Brei etwas sämiger.

NUTZEN

— Ideal als Babynahrung geeignet und für Menschen, die nicht mehr gut kauen können

Das Rezept kann in allen diesen Küchengeräten zubereitet werden. Breie aus dem Entsafter werden schonender verarbeitet!

Apfel-Banane-Mango-Brei

Zutaten für 1 Portion Brei

› *1 Mango*
› *1 Apfel*
› *1 Banane*

Zubereitung

Von der Mango die Schale und den Kern entfernen und die Frucht vierteln. Den Apfel waschen. Bei Bedarf das Kerngehäuse entfernen und den Apfel vierteln. Die Banane schälen und halbieren. Alle Zutaten in den Entsafter geben, bis eine schöne Konsistenz erreicht ist.

NUTZEN

— Vitaminbombe
— Ideal als Babynahrung geeignet und für Menschen, die nicht mehr gut kauen können

Das Rezept kann in allen diesen Küchengeräten zubereitet werden. Breie aus dem Entsafter werden schonender verarbeitet!

Süßkartoffel-Möhren-Brei

Zutaten für 1 Portion Brei

- *50 g Cashewkerne*
- *1 Süßkartoffel*
- *4 Möhren*

Zubereitung

Die Cashewkerne für mindestens 4 Stunden in Wasser einweichen. Danach das Wasser abgießen und die Cashewkerne spülen. Süßkartoffel und Möhren waschen. Süßkartoffel in Stücke und Möhren in Streifen schneiden. Alle Zutaten in den Entsafter geben. Die Mischung kann nach dem Entsaften kurz gekocht werden.

TIPP

Bei diesem Brei empfiehlt es sich, ein paar Tropfen Olivenöl einzurühren, damit die fettlöslichen Vitamine besser vom Körper aufgenommen werden können.

NUTZEN

— Vitaminbombe
— Ideal als Babynahrung geeignet und für Menschen, die nicht mehr gut kauen können

Das Rezept kann in allen diesen Küchengeräten zubereitet werden. Breie aus dem Entsafter werden schonender verarbeitet!